SAMUEL PEPYS IN PARIS
AND OTHER ESSAYS

UNIVERSITY OF NORTH CAROLINA
STUDIES IN THE ROMANCE LANGUAGES
AND LITERATURES

Number 24

SAMUEL PEPYS IN PARIS
AND OTHER ESSAYS

by

URBAN TIGNER HOLMES, JR.

CHAPEL HILL
THE UNIVERSITY OF NORTH CAROLINA PRESS

CONTENTS

A PREFACE

WITHIN THESE PAGES I have brought together three papers, or lectures as they should be called, which do not fit into the average philological journal. They try to "summon from the shadowy past the forms" that might have been, and in them controlled conjecture is permitted to stand beside proven facts. The first essay is intended to be the principal one and so it gives its title to the collection. It is representative of the methodology which I should like to see applied to certain other situations. For instance, we know precisely when Chaucer was in Italy, and I take it that we have a rather good idea of what was happening in the cities which he visited at that time. It would not be difficult to bring these elements together, as I have done for Samuel Pepys and Paris. The second lecture was written for a serious group of gardeners in Danville, Virginia. I have added to this and stiffened its material somewhat with notes. The third essay was delivered in several colleges of the State of Virginia in the year 1952-53, as a kind of epitome of my *Daily Living in the Twelfth Century* (University of Wisconsin Press, 1952, 1953).

I hope, dear reader, that your curiosity will be aroused by the methodology used in these three papers, and that you will "think it worth enjoying" and employing. For improvement in style and expression I am under great obligation to my editorial reader—*quae se semel tantum nominatam rursum mecum locuturam esse negat; idcirco hoc modo gratias ago.*

URBAN TIGNER HOLMES, JR.

SAMUEL PEPYS IN PARIS

I

SAMUEL PEPYS IN PARIS

THE READER might think from observing this title that we have discovered some continuation to the famous Diary which ends so abruptly on May 31st, 1669, three months before Pepys made his visit to the French capital. No papers of this kind have been found, of course, and yet it is not impossible to make this trip with our friend from Seething Lane to the Paris of September-October 1669, bearing in mind the sort of things which he liked to see, and making some very good guesses as to where he went and whom he met.

On August 21st, old style, 1669, Evelyn wrote to Pepys: "I could have set you down catalogues of many rare pictures and collections to be seen in that city [Paris], but you will every day meet with fresher intelligence. It is now many years since I was there *et mutantur tempora, et mores, et homines.* Pray forget not to visit the Taille-douce shops, and make collections of what they have excellent, especially the draughts of their palaces, churches and gardens, and the particulars you will have seen. They will greatly refresh you in your study and by your fireside, when you are many years returned. Israel, Sylvestre, Morin, Chaveau are great masters both for things of the kind extant, and inventions extremely pleasant. You will easily be acquainted with the best painters, especially Le Brun, who is the chief of them; and it would not be amiss to be present at their Academie, in which Monsieur Du Bosse (a principal member) will conduct you. For the rest I recommend you to God Almighty's protection; augure you a good journey, and kissing your ladies hands, remain. . . .

"These three letters I enclose to be presented according to the directions; with many more I could burthen you, but your short stay will not require it; and besides, being persons of great quality, much of your time would be consum'd in making and repaying but impertinent visits, in which I believe you would not willingly engage. I send you the letters open for you to seal when you please.

"P.S. Sr.—When you are arrived at Paris, the best service which can be done you, will be to address you where you may immediately repose yourself till you are provided and settled in a lodging suitable to your company. Therefore, you may please to enquire for one Hughs, an Englishman, who lives *à la Rue la*

Boucherie, au Fauxbourg St. Germain, a friend of Sr. S. Tuke's, who will assist you to Dr. Fritz Gerald, (to whom you have a letter) and he will assist you both to find out a fit lodging and whatever else you shall require."

This letter written by Evelyn was copied by Lord Braybrooke from the original in the collection of W. Upcott "of the London Institution." The note of thanks to Evelyn which Pepys wrote on his return to London, dating it November 2, o. s., 1669, was published by Lord Braybrooke from a copy among the papers of Samuel Pepys Cockerell:

"I beg you to believe I would not have been ten days returned into England without waiting on you, had it not pleased God to afflict mee by the sickness of my wife, who, from the first day of her coming back to London, hath layn under a fever so severe as at this hour to render her recoverie desperate; which affliction hath very much unfitted me for those acts of civilitie and respect which, amongst the first of my friends, I should have paid to yourselfe, as he to whom singly I owe the much greater part of the satisfaction I have met with in my late voyage. Next to you I have my acknowledgements to make to Sir Samuel Tuke, to whom (when in a condition of doing it) I shall beg your introducing me, for the owning of my obligations to him on the like behalfe . . ."

[Pepys records in the Diary for February 15th, 1669, that he saw Sir Samuel Tuke for the first time at a bookseller's. He found him conceited but eloquent. It is plain that two of the letters of introduction furnished by Evelyn and Tuke were to Dr. Fitz Gerald and to M. Abraham Bosse. We do not know to whom the third letter was addressed. Sir Samuel Tuke spent the period of the Protectorate abroad, and he was a favorite of Henrietta Maria, the Queen Mother of England, who was resident in France. Perhaps the third letter was to someone in her immediate *entourage.* We will assume for our purposes that it was to some distinguished person in Paris who was in a position to introduce the English traveller to the men of wit and learning. We will guess that it was for M. de Lamoignon, the first Président of Parlement, who was a leading patron of the best wits in Paris, and who received a circle of such people on Mondays.]

These two letters which we have reproduced in part are almost all that we have at our disposal for an understanding of Pepys's visit to France—almost, but not quite all. At the close of his life, in 1701, Pepys wrote again to Evelyn: ". . . through Holland and Flanders to Paris and so home—a tour that by the aid of your instructions I myselfe, when time was, and with a wife with me, dispatched in bare 2 [months]; and to a degree of satisfaction and solid usefulness that has stuck by mee through the whole course of my life and business since. . . ." This is striking evidence for the desirability of taking some account of what the Pepyses may have seen in the French capital. In another letter, addressed to John Brisbane, who was then in the French city, and written on March 12th, o. s., 1674, Samuel asks for a copy of the Gomboust map of Paris (1652), as well as a history of the city which he had tried in vain to buy on the spot, and he begs for some information on the French Navy to be secured from his friend, M. Mignon. In some additional letter material which was at the disposal of Mr. Bryant, Pepys tells us that his party left Paris for home on October 6th, o. s., and proceeded in leisurely fashion to Brussels—also that Balthazar St. Michel, his brother-in-law, accompanied Pepys and his wife throughout the journey, presumably to interpret when necessary and to serve in many other small ways.*

These details on the French journey are not numerous but they enable us to sketch in the background and outline. From the letter written after the return to London it is evident that Pepys was back in his office at Seething Lane by October 23rd, o. s. In 1701 he asserted that his travelling covered a bare two months, and Evelyn sent his "boat letter" on August 21st o. s. The departure from Holland to London can then be dated with reason as taking place on about August 24th. It will be noted that the Pepys family required from October 6th to October 23rd to make a leisurely return by way of the Low Countries. If their journey to Paris was made at approximately this same speed, we can assume that Paris was reached on September 10th or 11th. These dates are all given according to the old style used in England, and ten days must be added to each one if we are to compare events in Paris; the Pepys ménage spent in Paris the month extending from September 20th to October 16th, n. s., with some uncertainty as to the precision of the earlier of these dates.

---

* The curious reader will find a short note on sources at the end of this essay.

The reader will note that up to this point I have made frequent use of the auxiliaries "might" and "would." From now on I shall discard the expressions of doubt and probability, to permit greater ease in reading. The scholar will not forget to restore them if he seeks to weigh my assertions, and the evidence, for what they are truly worth.

We assume that the Pepyses came from Holland by way of Calais, as the Dutch traveller De Villers did in 1656. At that point they caught the Messagérie coach which conveyed them the rest of their journey to Paris. A six- or seven-day journey from Calais, even when spent in a rattling old conveyance by day, and at sundry inns by night, was sufficient to initiate the English traveller into some feeling for the country. Mrs. Pepys and her brother spoke French very well, and Samuel felt that he did too, by the time the Messagérie plodded into the little town of Saint-Denis, before making the last mile to the Paris gate. This point was reached at four o'clock in the afternoon, as travellers were nervous about approaching the outer limits of the city after nightfall. Highwaymen were not unknown. All along the way Pepys had been noticing that the roads in France were "paved with a small square freestone, so that the country does not much molest the traveler with dirt and ill way, as in England, only 'tis somewhat hard to the poor horses' feet, which causes them to ride more temperately, seldom going out of the trot, or *grand pas,* as they call it." (The words are those of Evelyn from an entry made in 1644 in his Diary.) After leaving Beaumont, the last night stop on the road, the travellers realized that they were getting near to Paris "seeing the number of fine houses which were scattered about the countryside. The villages through which we passed were now larger and better built." (De Villers had also commented in his account that the city noises became evident between Saint-Denis and the city gate.)

The Calais coach rumbled to a stop before the *Ecu Dauphin* on the Rue Bourg-l'Abbé, which was the terminus of the service from Boulogne, Montreuil, and Calais. This short street was one block east of the Rue Saint-Denis and just west of the Rue Saint-Martin. Pepys secured a temporary lodging at this hostelry where he was able to leave Mrs. Pepys and this arrangement permitted him and "Balty" to adjust their attire before calling upon Hughs and Dr. Fitz Gerald. As he made his toilet we can hear a contemptuous word or two from Samuel on the ridiculousness of the long doublets worn by the French, their large *cravates*, and their peculiar wigs. "Balty" only smiled. The Fauxbourg Saint-Germain was at this time the quarter which attracted travellers of the Protestant faith. They lived there in large numbers: Dutchmen, Germans, and Englishmen, although the temple to which they went on Sundays was at Charenton, two leagues beyond the Porte Saint-Antoine at the very opposite end of Paris. This fact accounts for the residence of Hughs on the Rue de la Boucherie; but we must remember also that the medical schools were there, and that will explain the presence of Dr. Fitz Gerald. Since the only address that Hughs seemed to need was Rue de la Boucherie, and as Evelyn did not prefix a title to the name, we assume that he was a well-known tradesman in that area.

The street of Bourg-l'Abbé, as the map of Jacques Gomboust (1652) shows plainly, was one block east of the Rue Saint-Denis, which was a main artery. Pepys reached this latter street by way of the "savory" Rue des Ours which entered the artery at the very point where the Rue Mauconseil entered it from the opposite direction. Pepys asked the coachman about the Hôtel de Bourgogne and its scheduled performances as his eye tried to catch sight of the theatre, which was hidden from his gaze by a bend in the Rue Mauconseil. His coach descended the Rue Saint-Denis as far as the Rue de la Ferronerie, where it turned right with intent to cross the river by the Pont Neuf. The coachman was instructed by his energetic little passenger to call at the General Post on the Rue des Bourdonnoys, where he could inquire for mail. We may quote De Villers for this: "We left [the street of Saint-Denis] at the place where it joins that of the Ferronerie. This last runs beside the charnal houses of the Holy Innocents, and is remarkable because almost all the iron merchants, the brass, copper and tin smiths, have their shops there. We were pointed out the well where the traitor Ravaillac hid before killing Henry IV. As we reached the Rue Saint-Honoré, we turned down the Rue Bourdonnois and thus reached the Point Neuf."

The Pont Neuf attracted much comment from Pepys. The view of the city, which was visible up and down the river, and the broad area of the bridge, which was *not* lined with houses, were startling. "There is one passage for coaches, and two for foot passengers three or four feet higher, and of convenient breadth for eight or ten to go abreast. On the middle of this stately bridge . . . stands the famous statue of Henry the Great on horseback . . . The place where it is erected is inclosed with a strong and beautiful grate of iron about which there are always mountebanks showing their feats to the idle passengers." (These are the words of Evelyn.) As Pepys crossed the Pont he noted "the vast number of boats, of wood, hay, charcoal, corn, wine and other commodities." Once he was over the bridge, the Rue Dauphine, broad and straight, led directly to the Porte Dauphine, and from there the house which Pepys was seeking was only about two short blocks away. Like Dr. Lister (who was in Paris in 1698) Pepys as he rode along was impressed with Parisian houses "built of hewn stone entirely" or "whited over with plaister." The lower windows of all houses were "grated with strong bars of iron; which must be a vast expense." He noted, as Lister did, that "the streets are paved with a very hard sand stone, about eight inches square."

The very *fiacre* in which Samuel was riding excited his curiosity—a vehicle with front wheels unusually small ("not above two feet and a half diameter") having a low coach-box which made it easier to have a clear view over the coachman's head. Coaches were built in this way to enable them to turn easily through the crowded streets. Lister noted that these Paris coaches had double springs at each corner, which made for comfortable riding. Pepys certainly noticed this same thing. Pepys, like Lister, was attracted by the strange appearance of the throng of people in the streets: the many monks in their habits, the "counsellors and the chief officers of the courts of justice . . . they and their wives have their trains carried up; so there are abundance to be seen walking about the streets in this manner." Then there were the many beggars. "The great multitude of poor wretches in all parts of the city is such, that a man in a coach, a-foot, in the shop, is not able to do any business for the numbers and importunities of beggars; and to hear their miseries is very lamentable; and if you give to one you immediately bring a whole swarm upon you." The coaches were very numerous in the narrow streets and "passengers a-foot no ways secured from the hurry and danger of coaches, which always passing the streets with an air of haste, and a full trot upon broad flat stones, betwixt high and large resounding houses, make a sort of music which should seem very agreeable to the Parisians."

After Pepys had descended at the establishment of Hughs he sent in his card and was seen in due course. From there he was conducted immediately to the lodging of Dr. Fitz Gerald whom, by lucky accident, he found at home. It was at this point that our "curious" friend began to note the lack of conveniences in the French houses: (to quote Dr. Lister once more) "many utensils and conveniences of life are wanting here, which we in England have. This makes me remember what Monsieur Justell, a Parisian formerly, told me here [in London], that he had made a catalogue of near threescore things of this nature which they wanted in Paris."

From Fitz Gerald Pepys soon learned the latest intelligence of what was happening in Paris and the world. Molière had played *Tartuffe* on Friday, September 13th, but was now gone to Chambord with the Court and would not return until late in October, probably too late for Mr. Pepys to attend one of his performances. The English Queen Mother, Henrietta Maria, had died on September 10th, n. s. Her body would be carried from the Convent at Chaillot to the Basilica of Saint-Denis on Sunday, the 22nd, starting an hour after sundown, and the procession would be lighted by a hundred pages carrying torches. This information electrified Pepys. He was after all obligated to Sir Samuel Tuke for his references in Paris, and Sir Samuel had been closely associated with the household of the Queen Mother. Queen Henrietta had left London and Somerset House for good on June 24th, 1665, and retired to her chateau at Colombes on the outskirts of Paris. Pepys knew that news of her death would be received in London with considerable mourning. Here was he, a British crown official—one of the comparatively small group of official Englishmen who chanced to be in Paris. On his return to London he would be asked about this funeral in detail. He expressed to Fitz Gerald his desire to be among the first mourners, and Fitz Gerald understood. "Balty" St. Michel must have had other thoughts as he listened to this discourse. His father had gone to England, attached to Queen Henrietta Maria's household. He had been dropped because of his interest in the Reformed religion and had been living in poverty in London ever since. "Balty" did not burden the company with these thoughts.

Just where Dr. Fitz Gerald found a lodging for the Pepys couple and their brother St. Michel is something we shall never know. The Rue de Tournon was noted for its excellent hostelries in the Saint-Germain Quarter. A room nicely hung with tapestries, with three beds and other adequate furnishings, cost about 15 crowns a month. Pepys and his wife were quite comfortable in such a room, with a small antechamber adjoining. For a time "Balty" had a shakedown prepared for him in the antechamber, but he soon took to sharing a bed with another single gentleman in a chamber nearby. Pepys learned, as Lister did thirty year later, that one could rent "coaches *de Remise*, by the month, which are very well gilt, neat harness, and good horses: and these all strangers hire by the day or month, at about three crowns English a day." Pepys engaged one for his stay, which gave him the means of getting about Paris easily under the guidance of an experienced coachman and of enjoying the parks. Fitz Gerald, with some show of amusement, told his guest that Mr. Evelyn had been ill informed in supplying him with a letter for M. Abraham Bosse to facilitate a presentation at the Académie de Peinture. M. Bosse had been expelled from that body since 1662, which made him the last man who could gracefully introduce Pepys to Le Brun and to his former colleagues. As Bosse was a marvellous etcher, Samuel was anxious to call upon him for that reason alone. He had too much tact to show the letter which requested that Bosse should present the bearer at the sessions of the Académie.

In the Diary for January 25th, 1669 Pepys recorded his special fondness for collecting portraits executed by the engraver Robert Nanteuil. He managed a visit to the atelier of this master of psychology and, as he reported in a letter to John Brisbane, "recruited [himself] with . . . the heads of persons of quality cut by Nanteuil, and this not only within the circle of the Court and camp, but more especially with heads of admirals or other sea-captains. . . ." He found the artist to be a vigorous man in his forties "with a most cunning eye for pourtraiture, so that he do look into the very soul of him whom he draws" (in words which I am putting into Pepys's mouth).

Our traveller felt the need of expert guidance in his search for what was best in *taille-douce*, and so he managed an introduction to one of the most distinguished connoisseurs of the graphic arts. He was presented to the famous collector Michel

de Marolles, Abbé de Villeloin. In words which we will imagine:
"Today did call with M. du Bosse at the lodging of M. de Marolles,
the collector of stamps. We found him in his priest's clothing,
a mild old man, whose eyes do light up before a volume of drawings and stamps as those of some would kindle before a fine
dinner. It is now two years since he did dispose of his collection to the King's Cabinet. I am told that this did consist of
123,400 pieces, bound into 400 large and 120 small tomes. More
than six hundred master *tailleurs* were found in this collection.
With the money thus gained the old man is now starting anew.
He receives many tradesmen with stamps and drawings to sell
and he had a brave pile on a table in his closet when we made
our visit. Some he showed me which I too must buy. He will
take me with him some day to call upon the sellers." Even
though Pepys did not make a formal appearance at a meeting of
the Académie de Peinture, he called at the shop maintained by
the Académie in its quarters at the Palais Brion in the Palais
Royal; and he attended for a brief session one of the sketching
classes held at the Académie on Thursday afternoons, where the
students were engaged in sketching a male figure.

As an enthusiastic member of the Royal Academy of Science
in London, which met at Gresham College, Samuel had a definite
longing to be present at a session of the Académie Royale des
Sciences in Paris, which met every Wednesday and Saturday
from 3 to 5 P.M. in the Bibliothèque du Roy on the Rue Vivienne.
With chagrin he learned from Fitz Gerald that the Académie
(only three years old) did not meet during September and
October. Fitz Gerald proposed to present Pepys to the Abbé de
Bourzeis, member of the French Academy, who was also chief
founder of the Académie des Sciences and a great intellectual
figure in Paris. Then they learned that the Abbé, who was
sixty-three years of age, had gone for the warm months to his
Abbey of Saint-Martin de Cores. The sessions at the home of
Bourzeis were known as *petites académies*.

Though the Académie sessions were not being held, it was at
least possible to visit the Bibliothèque Royale, provided permis-
sion for the visit was secured. Pepys had no difficulty in getting this. He found that the library, installed on the Rue de
Vivienne since 1666 (to which address it had moved from the
Rue de la Harpe), was still in the throes of arrangement. A
score of rooms were filled with printed books and manuscripts,

and there were also museum antiquities and natural science collections. He was told that the books and collections which were of more immediate use to the King remained housed in the Louvre. Pepys was shown the Greek manuscript of Dioscorides and the handsome manuscript of the Hymns of Prudentius (which were viewed by Lister also, thirty years later). As he gazed at the fine manuscript of the Epistles he muttered under his breath and remarked later to Mrs. Pepys: " 'Tis indeed a part of our Cambridge manuscript which hath the Gospels in a find bold hand. I fain would have₁ laid my hands on their part to join it with ours, but I was not *much* tempted as I had not the opportunity."

Some ten days after the Clerk of the Acts was lodged in Paris he received a visit from M. Mignon, one of the *conseillers du Roy, d'état et de la marine,* who was accompanied by the *Greffier* of the Paris Naval Office. The *Greffier* was in fact Pepys's opposite number in the French Navy, but Pepys remarked after his visitors left: "I could not own that, God helpe me, as he seemed a person of far less consequence than I holde myself to be." Samuel had already made the acquaintance of M. Mignon, who had been Secretary to M. Colbert when the latter was Ambassador in London. Colbert had been Minister of the French Navy since March of 1669. Pepys could only approve of this in his heart, as he knew that like himself "Colbert was a great man for business," but he had had some adverse comment to make to his brother-in-law when he learned from some one in Paris that the little Comte de Vermandois, "a puling brat, the King's bastard," was newly created Admiral of France. M. Mignon reassured his English friend's tactful inquiries on this subject. There were two new Vice-admirals—a new departure— who would actually command the eastern and western fleets. The *greffier* remarked that his office was at that very moment engaged in preparing a new set of *règlements* for the governing of the fleets and that these regulations would be published in November. Pepys was all ears for this. He made suggestions and he was most pleased when it was proposed to him that he should pay a visit to the Admiralty Office in the Palais, where his ideas could be given further attention.

Pepys was flattered that his competence "was owned even by our adversaries," but he suspected that he would not be drawn very far into the French confidence. Probably he sensed that

Colbert had big plans for the rejuvenation of the French Navy which involved playing the British off against the Dutch and extending French hegemony to the Rhine. In doing this the French were not apt to neglect paying social amenities to the busiest little man in the Navy Office at Seething Lane. This professional call was returned by Pepys very promptly. He saw M. Mignon at his house; he visited the *greffier* at the *Greffe de la Marine*. Pepys's mind was all set for comparisons. He thought their number of clerks was excessive, but he did like the models of their ships, which were "graceful and excellent in design." As he saw the Office busy at work, he wished that he could slow up their efficiency a bit by giving them that troublesome colleague of his at Seething Lane, Sir John Minnes.

Not many days were allowed to pass before our traveller paid a visit in the company of Dr. Fitz Gerald, to La Charité and the Hôtel Dieu, to observe the cutting for the stone. "There great numbers are cut yearly . . . in both of these are wired chests full of stones cut from human bodies; and in the chest of La Charité is one, which exceeds all belief; it was cut from a monk who died in the operation; it is as big as a child's head. It is only the model or pattern of the stone which is kept in the chest. . . ." (Dr. Lister also reported that one persistent operator performed the operation "upon nine persons in three quarters of an hour, very dexterously.") Evelyn witnessed such an operation at La Charité in 1650: "A child of eight or nine years old underwent the operation with most extraordinary patience, and expressing great joy when he saw the stone was drawn." Pepys observed (as Evelyn did) : ". . . the Charité gave me great satisfaction, in seeing how decently and christianly the sick people are attended, even to delicacy. I have seen them served by noble persons, men and women. They have also gardens, walks and fountains." Although May was the favored month for cutting for the stone, emergency cases could be handled at any time.

Venereal disease was very prevalent in Paris at this period. There were many bills posted in the Fauxbourg Saint-Germain, whether because this was the medical center or because the quack doctors found a good trade among the foreigners, we cannot say. To quote Lister: "more particularly in the Fauxbourgh of St. Germain, the quack's bills printed in great uncial letters: De par l'ordre du Roy. Remède infaillible et commode pour la guérison des maladies secrètes sans garder la chambre." Samuel, despite his leanings toward pretty women, was considerably deterred by the evidence afforded in such advertising. He had cause to remark on several occasions: "She was a pretty black girl and I doubt not I could have offered further. I feared to offer her a baiser, suspecting that she too was full of the pox." Lister insisted thirty years later that Paris had no remedies that were not used in England, and that England had something not so systematically practiced in Paris: continence.

Pepys avoided the drinking of Paris water. "The river water is very pernicious to all strangers, not the French excepted, that come from any distance, but not to the natives of Paris, causing looseness and sometimes disenteries. . . . As for the spring water from the Maison des Eaux [terminus of the aquaduct from Arcueil], it is wholesome in this respect, and keeps the body firm but it is very apt to give the stone," Lister remarked. Pepys sometimes took chocolate for his morning draught. The chocolate shop of David Chaliou was established at the corner of the Rue Saint-Honoré and l'Arbre-Sec, close by the Croix du Tiroir. This was an excellent stand, and especially so when malefactors were broken on the wheel at that intersection and the crowd was very thick. Chaliou had the Royal privilege and monopoly for dispensing chocolate until 1674. In Paris the Faculty of Medicine had given approval to the strange drink since 1661, but the best society was divided on the subject of its medicinal virtues. Pepys was all the more keen on taking chocolate since he found that the value of the drink was a subject for discussion. He was never a man to avoid that sort of experiment.

Pepys had his first introduction to coffee also at this time. The Faculty of Medicine was still silent on the value of this drink. Those who sold it were Armenians who had a few booths, and who travelled about the streets with their small tray of cups strapped before them and a pot of coffee in hand, Oriental style. (That very autumn, after Pepys had returned to London, Soliman Aga, envoy from Turkey, began to popularize the use of coffee in Paris. Our friend missed this Oriental gentleman by a month.) The coffee which Pepys drank was bitter, without sugar and somewhat thick because of the pulverized grounds. His comment was: "This morning I did try for my morning draught some of the Turkey drink called *cahve*. We took it from a filthy fellow dressed in turban and full breeches who stopped us on the way. I found it bitter and am ready to agree with those who say it hath little use for health." He asked for tea at the shop of a *limonadier* in the Palais Royal. Ale houses were quite plentiful and Pepys stepped into many of them in the course of his visit. Indeed, Lister later remarked on this habit in Paris: "Sure I am the Parisians, both men and women, are strangely altered in their constitutions and habit of body; from lean and slender, they are become fat and corpulent, the women especially; which, in my opinion, can proceed from nothing so much as the daily drinking strong liquors." Norman cider was another drink that Pepys enjoyed. He found it "as sweet as new wine," again in the words of Lister.

The Pepyses were lodged in the Fauxbourg Saint-Germain. It was very rare for lodgers to arrange for meals with the proprietor of their hotel. It was quite common, on the other hand, for a group of friends to make common cause of their resources and eat regularly in the antechamber of one of their number who was blessed with sufficient space and kitchen privileges. They hired the cook and attendants between them and divided the costs of food. Pepys, his wife, and "Balty" we will suppose, were admitted to the circle which was shared by Fitz Gerald. On many occasions too they went to such taverns as the Ile de France on the Rue Guénégaud, the Beuf et les trois chandeliers on the Rue de la Huchette, and the Coq hardi on the Rue Saint-André-des-arts. There were some sixty taverns in Paris where one could find food, but many were not of a high class. Pepys noted that eating at such taverns was quite dear; he estimated that it would cost a person some hundred and twenty livres a month (£ 5. 5 s.). The livre was equivalent to ten-pence half-penny.

At this date Paris had some great connoisseurs of cuisine: the *goulus* and the *friands*. Those with whom Pepys dined knew of these circles and jested about them. There was, above all, the group which dined at the house of the Marquise de Sablé, hard by the Convent of Port-Royal. Our friend was curious, but he made no effort to get an invitation, suspecting that this would not be easy. After all, he was no *gourmet*. He asked only that the meat should be clean and decently prepared. He had considerable fault to find with French food, more censure than praise. He tried *pain de Gonesse* and pronounced it too stale. *Pain coquillé* was good, resembling the Dutch buns sold in England, which were even better. The ordinary *pain mollet*, or best white bread on the table, tasted bitter (as Lister found it). The grey salt which was served excited his attention.

The prevalence of long turnips, of carrots, red cabbage, onions, garlic, leeks, and shallots—the fondness for Roman lettuce, white beets, and asparagus—also brought some comment from his lips. He was not particularly fond of the potato in London, but he thought he missed it on the Paris tables. He observed, as did Lister, that the French were partial to vegetable soups. He regretted that mushrooms were not in season and he was desirous of getting some of the stewed oysters, which were marketed, he was told, in a dried state, laid in straw baskets. He found the veal "red and coarse" and all the French meat was "leaner and more dry," inclined to be "high." (It will be remembered at this point what Pepys thought of the "stinking meat" of the William Penn establishment.) To quote once more from Lister: "the air of France being so much drier, keeping of meat not only makes it tender, but improves the taste." Pepys did not say "amen" to this.

He liked the French marmalade made of "orange flowers, the juice of lemons and fine sugar." He enjoyed the Vattee, consisting of "muscat wine distilled with citron pills and orange flowers," and the strong water, rataphia, delighted him for after dinner. But above all the variety of strange foods, Pepys and his wife took delight in the gay company that gathered around the table. The dining room was makeshift, with none of the fine appurtenances which Pepys enjoyed in his apartment at the Navy office, but the talk was witty, though somewhat medical and critical, and there was considerable deference paid to the representative of the Royal Navy and his lady. She, because of her French origin, was more often than not the subject of gentle twitting and chaffing. "Balty" said little; his role was a minor one.

It was a considerable disappointment for the two Pepyses that Molière was not in Paris. To miss *Tartuffe* by less than a week! Today we do not have the programs of the Marais Theatre and of the Hôtel de Bourgogne for those weeks in September and October. We will assume that the couple saw a few performances at the two theatres, although they were again informed that the season for the theatre would not really open

until the first part of November. Floridor put on at the Hôtel
de Bourgogne a performance of Montfleury's *Procès de la Femme
Juge et Partie*. Pepys kept hoping to see also the play con-
cerned, the *Femme Juge et Partie* by the same author, but he
had no luck. From the *Procès* he was not impressed with the
possibilities of the other. Hauteroche's *Le souper mal apprêté*
was also performed. Pepys had very little that was favorable
to say about the actresses—La Beauchasteau, La Villiers, and
D'Hennebault. But when he saw Rosimond's *Le Nouveau Festin
de Pierre* and Visé's *Les intrigues de la lotterie* at the Marais,
he was charmed by La Champmeslé. He rather contemplated
securing an introduction to her, but no one took him up on his
suggestion, so he allowed the thought to pass. The Hôtel de
Bourgogne he found too small and somewhat rickety. He commented upon the fact that the Marais was even worse, for it had
not been intended for a theatre in the first place and it was in
that part of town where one's nostrils caught an occasional
whiff of the town drain. Molière's hall at the Palais Royal he
understood to be larger and much finer, "being constructed not
so many years back for the proper housing of plays." He was
especially annoyed by the slowness which the French theatres
exercised in starting their performances. To announce a play
for three-thirty and begin at five-thirty was indeed something
not to be tolerated, and the "people were unmannerly. Indeed
the people of quality do act more unseemly than those of the
parterre."

Mrs. Pepys accompanied her husband to the theatre and on
some of his visits (when she was really there as a sort of inter-
preter). For the most part, however, she behaved like the
average French lady of the day and remained in her bedroom
and closet. It was the custom for a lady to receive her visitors
as she lay on the bed. Soon after reaching Paris, Samuel hired
a young woman as maid and companion for his wife. The girl
slept on a bed at the foot of the one which the Pepyses occupied.
During the day she waited on Mrs. Pepys, furnished her with
the latest gossip, and ran errands. In the evenings it was sometimes her duty to comb the master's hair. He was not above
stealing a kiss or so, if his wife was in the antechamber, and he
commented upon the "slyness of these French minxes." It was
a perpetual concern to have enough fresh linen, as the travellers
did not have sufficient luggage to accommodate much of this.

The maid knew a laundress, who came by for the linen on one occasion when she was summoned. Pepys was somewhat amused to think that his linen was washed in the Seine from one of those little boats moored perpetually at the abreuvoir Macon. He observed that they kept the river somewhat foul at that spot and he was glad he personally did not have to venture into one of them.

Once a week both husband and wife read the *Gazette* of Loret, and Mrs. Pepys was reading one of the latest romances. Perhaps this was *La promenade de Versailles* by Mlle de Scudéry, although she had at hand also a copy of *Mathilde d'Aguilar*, by the same author, into which she dipped now and then.

Both the Pepyses were somewhat intrigued by the marvellous seamless boots which Nicolas Lestage, now the King's shoemaker, had devised. They were also amused by the number of poems which were being written on this subject. Mrs. Pepys was conveyed frequently in the family's rented coach to call at the *couturières* who sold underclothing. Pepys was persuaded to buy her a few petticoats and a camisole from Mmes Rémond and Prévot of the Rue des Petits-Champs. Outer dresses were still manufactured by the men *tailleurs*. As he desired the very best for her, Mrs. Pepys was taken by her husband to Bandelet, the Queen's tailor, who lived on the Rue Richelieu (in the very house where Molière was to pass away, five years later).

When his lady asked to go to Martial, the great glover and perfumer, Pepys was more stubborn. A dozen gloves were a small matter, even perfumed ones, but Martial sold other things—Spanish white (white of lead), Spanish rouge (red lead), alum, distilled vinegar, beef bile, almond water, pommade des pieds de veau—which were known to have most deleterious effects. On these occasions Pepys suggested that his wife should confine her beauty aids to milk and early morning dew. Paris was famous for the manufacture of garters. Samuel's coach took his wife to the sign of the Cross on the Rue d'Arnetal, where the best of these were sold. But the place that delighted both of them was the Halle aux toiles where fine linen could be purchased. Linen from Normandy, Brittany, and Flanders was a delight to those who appreciated good lace. On one occasion Pepys took a look at la Fripperie, the second-hand clothing mart which was near the *halles*. In a long stone gallery the second-hand merchants cried their wares: "Bon manteau de campagne,"

"Beau justaucorps." One had only to glance in their direction
and he was pulled in. De Villers advised against buying there
as they could make the "old look like new; so skilled were they
in patching."

What Mrs. Pepys enjoyed best were the drives and walks in
the fine gardens and parks. The Luxembourg garden was just
a stone's throw from their lodging on the Rue de Tournon. They
often walked there of an evening. The finest outing was in the
Cours de la Reine, which was approached from the Gate of the
Tuileries on the right bank of the Seine. "It was constructed
at the behest of Marie de Medicis . . . it consists of four rows of
trees, 1600 paces in length, surrounded by a moat, and on the
side facing the river by a very low wall. . . . One enters by a
large gate guarded by a porter with a lodge nearby. In the
middle of the cours is a large circle, to which all the drives lead,
where carriages can turn. There is another gate at the opposite
end." This is the description given by De Villers. Lister says
of it: "The middle alley holds four lines of coaches at least, and
each side alley two apiece; these eight lines of coaches, may
when full, supposing them to contain near eighty coaches apiece,
amount to about six or seven hundred. On the field side, joining
close to the alleys of the coaches, there are several acres of
meadow planted with trees, well grown, into narrow alleys in
quicunx order, to walk in the grass, if any have a mind to light;
and this must needs be very agreeable in the heats of summer. . . .
You are confined to your line; and oftentimes, the princes of the
blood coming in, and driving at pleasure, make a strange stop
and embarras . . . if the weather has been rainy, there is no
driving in it, it is so miry and ill gravelled." To quote further
from Lister: "Towards eight or nine o'clock . . . most of them
[the coaches] return from the Cours, and [their occupants] land
at the garden gate of the Tuileries, where they walk in the cool
of the evening." The middle walk of the Tuileries garden was
considered the most memorable thing in Paris during the warm
season. The Tuileries "has shaded terraces on two sides, one
along the River Seine, planted with trees, very diverting, with
great parterres in the middle, and large fountains of water
which constantly play; one end is the front of that magnificent
palace the Louvre; the other is low, and for prospects, open to
the fields."

The Bois de Boulogne was not very far beyond the Cours de la

Reine. One had only to drive past Chaillot. This lovely park, planted with oaks, was formerly a favorite place for duels, which gave it considerable romantic flavor in the eyes of Pepys. In the midst of it was a large crossroads with a stone cross in the center. On one occasion our English traveller descended there and walked with his lady to the royal house named Madrid, which was built by Francis I in imitation of the castle in Madrid where he was a prisoner after the Battle of Pavia. The Pepyses found the place in ruin, which seemed a shame, "because it was quite fair." Not more than half a league away from this was the drill field at Neuilly where the royal Musketeers were wont to drill.

Dr. Fitz Gerald took the couple to the Jardin du Roy in the Fauxbourg Saint-Victor where the medical students studied plants. In the middle of this was an elaborate sundial and a fountain which discharged its water in a basin surrounded by cypress trees. The Garden was in charge of the King's senior physician, and Fitz Gerald offered to escort Pepys upstairs to the dissecting room, for research in anatomy was constantly going on in the buildings in the grounds. Pepys was "strongly tempted by love of that which is new and strange," but he thought the better of it on third and fourth thought—and declined.

On nearly every Sunday Pepys, with his wife and "Balty," went to the Protestant Temple at Charenton. It was "a very fair and spacious room, built of freestone, very decently adorned with paintings of the Tables of Law, the Lord's Prayer, and Creed. The pulpit stands at the upper end in the middle, having an enclosure of seats about it, where the Elders and persons of greatest quality and strangers sit; the rest of the congregation on forms, and low stools, but none in pews. . . . I was greatly pleased with their harmonious singing of the Psalms, which they all learn perfectly well, their children being as duly taught these, as their catechism." (The words are Evelyn's.) Pepys contrived without much difficulty to secure places near to the pulpit. The sermon, in a language that was some effort for him to comprehend, was dull, and he began to regret his pride in securing a place from which he could not "slip away with honor." Pepys was aware too of the sullen looks which the populace gave the carriages that returned from the prêche. He was a little disturbed by this, but he was determined "to show that an Eng-

lishman cannot be faced down by such scurvie knaves!" On
several occasions he stepped into Nôtre Dame and other well
known churches. He climbed to the top of the tower of Saint-
Jacques de la Boucherie and gazed over the roofs of the city,
which he found "fair, but not stretching so far into the distance
as those of London town." Samuel did not forget to visit the
University, which he found to consist of no fewer than sixty-
five colleges. But he agreed with Evelyn that "they in nothing
approach ours at Oxford [and Cambridge] for state and order."
He "entered into some of the schools" and "found a grave Doctor
in his chair, with a multitude of auditors, who all write as he
dictates; and this they call a course." He too admired the res-
torations made by Richelieu at the Sorbonne—especially the
"sumptuous church."

The Louvre was a place of special interest, particularly the
long gallery which extended from the Louvre proper to the
Tuileries Palace. "Under this . . . dwell goldsmiths, painters,
statuaries, and architects, who being the most famous for their
art in Christendom have stipends allowed them by the King."
(We are quoting Evelyn.) De Villers describes the Royal Press
which was at the Tuileries end of the gallery "There are five
large rooms, fully arched, in one of which are five presses where
they print the books. The other rooms are used for drying sheets
of paper and for storing the completed books. The type setting
room is on the floor above the printery. They were not working
so strenuously there as down below." On this ground floor of
the long gallery "before each door there is a name plate of the
name of the master working there." Pepys followed the example
of Evelyn and bought several classics at the Royal Press. He
returned to the Louvre proper through another gallery "where
hung the pictures of all the kings and queens and prime nobility
of France." From there he went down into the Salle des An-
tiques and saw the marble figures, including the Diana—also
the "huge globe suspended by chains."

Philipps Lebas, the scientific instrument maker, was about to
move to the gallery of the Louvre, Pepys found, but he saw him
still in his old quarters. Lebas showed him the latest in glasses
for seeing the very small, and Pepys inquired of him whether he
had any device that would help his ailing sight. "He could do
no more than Greatorex." Samuel, alas, was not much inter-
ested in reading at the time, in doubt as he was about his sight,

but he visited the booksellers. There was Thomas Moette on the Rue de la Vieille Boucherie, near Saint-Jacques, who sold rare volumes. Frédéric Léonard at the sign of the Venetian shield on the Rue Saint-Jacques made a specialty of diplomatic subjects and political theory. Books were rather expensive. As Lister remarked: "I was at an auction of books in the Rue Saint-Jacques, where there were about forty or fifty people, most abbots and monks. The books were sold with a great deal of trifling and delay as with us, and very dear." Pepys wanted a copy of the Gomboust map, and also the *Théâtre des Antiquitez de Paris* of Jacques du Breul.

The King's musicians were with him at Chambord; but Pepys heard François Couperin, the organist at Saint-Gervais. Some lutists and a player on the theorbo came on invitation to Pepys's lodging, but he found them not of the best. He visited Nicolas Chéron, the maker of musical instruments, and commented favorably upon his skill.

There were various people in Paris whom Pepys contrived to see for brief visits. There was Raveneau, the expert on forgery, whose book on this subject (printed in 1665) was arousing so much attention that it was suppressed by Parlement four months after the Pepys *ménage* was back in London. The expert on codes, Louis Rossignol, was worthy of a visit. Pepys had made a practice of composing ciphers and he liked to talk with a man who could break them. He found Rossignol "old and somewhat doddering."

Mrs. Pepys was anxious to see Mlle de Scudéry of the Rue de Beauce, in the Marais district, but this estimable lady was out of town, and Samuel remarked to himself: "I was glad thereof as I can not abide long wind, and I was afeared her speech might be like that of her romances." The visit at the house of Président Lamoignon was a memorable occasion, where our "curious friend" was pleased "that they did do him much honor." This was followed the next week by an invitation to the Wednesday assembly at the house of Gilles Ménage in the Cloister Nôtre Dame. "Strange that he should be so quarrelsome, to be at odds with Chapelain, Molière and Boileau, and most of the men of wit of this day, and yet he seemeth mild-mannered enough, although somewhat dull and conceited." This circle of acquaintance was pursued no further. The French men of wit and learning were polite to Samuel as to a distinguished foreigner, but he had nothing further to offer them.

As mid-October approached, in the French style of reckoning, the Pepys family knew that they must soon be back in London. They had but a scant two months to devote to their continental journey. In coming they had travelled by coach through Calais, Boulogne, and Beauvais. Samuel wanted to see as much as possible; so it was decided—by him—to return in the Brussels coach, which would carry them into Flanders by way of Senlis, La Ferté, Guise, L'Isle, Tournay, and Douay. The *carosses de route* for Brussels left on Wednesdays and Saturdays from the *Grand Cerf* in the Rue Saint-Denis. In order to allow for a leisurely journey, Wednesday, October 16th, was the latest advisable date. This meant that they would not be able to attend the service in honor of Henrietta Maria at Chaillot, where Bossuet, the Bishop of Condom, would deliver the oration. Pepys was not too sorry. At that time the name of Bossuet was not yet famed for eloquence and Samuel occasionally found himself fed up with the men of the cloth.

Ormesson has recorded in his *Mémoires* that the weather at that time in Paris was unsually hot and dry. Mrs. Pepys drank a glass of cool water before the departure of the coach for the north. As they reached Brussels she was already suffering from a fever. When they finally came to rest in Seething Lane she was dangerously ill with what we suspect was typhoid. The "French idyll" was at an end.

Since the character of this paper is only semi-learned, I do not wish to burden the reader with notes. The first two letters in question have been published most recently as Nos. 33 and 34 in R. G. Howarth's *Letters and the Second Diary of Samuel Pepys* (London, 1932). Evelyn actually wrote out a list of the things which Pepys should see in France (especially Paris). This list was printed by Clara Marburg, no. 18 in the Appendix of her *Mr. Pepys and Mr. Evelyn* (London, 1935). The letter written in 1701 was published by J. R. Tanner in the *Private Correspondence and Miscellaneous Papers of Samuel Pepys*, (New York, 1925). Vol. II; the letter to Brisbane is printed by J. R. Tanner in his *Further Correspondence of Samuel Pepys* (London, 1929). See also Arthur Bryant's *Samuel Pepys, the Man in the Making* (London, 1933) for the additional data on the French journey.

I have used many books on Paris and French life in the 17th century. Prominent among these are: "A Journey to Paris in the Year 1698," by Dr. Martin Lister, printed in John Pinkerton's *Voyages and Travels* (Philadelphia, 1911), Vol. IV; *The Diary of John Evelyn*, ed. William Bray (St. Dunstan Society, Akron, Ohio, 1901); [De Villers], *Journal d'un Voyage à Paris*, ed. A. P. Faugère (Paris, 1862); Emile Magne, *Images de Paris sous Louis XIV* (Paris, 1939); *Le livre commode des addresses de Paris pour 1692*, ed. E. Fournier (Paris, 1878), and other volumes in the Elzevir series; pertinent volumes in A. Franklin, *La vie privée d'autrefois* (Paris, 1888-1903), and so on.

MEDIAEVAL GARDENS

II

MEDIAEVAL GARDENS

I T MAY SEEM presumptuous on my part to write on this topic
in one brief paper when others have treated it more at length.[1]
But the experts have usually lumped together a span of from five
hundred to a thousand years, and because the miniatures and
descriptions are plentiful from the fifteenth and sixteenth centuries, attention has been focussed there. My concern will be
with gardens of the period that I know best, the twelfth and
thirteenth centuries, although I must draw slightly on a description of the ninth century garden of St. Gall, and for two
generalities I will be obliged to the later material gathered by
Sir Frank Crisp.

Albertus Magnus (1193-1280) gives us a precise description
of the ideal layout of a garden in his day.[2] Within a wall there
shall be a fine stretch of lawn,. At the southern end near the
wall there should be trees: pear, apple, pomegrantes, laurels,
cypress, and other species, together with vines which will give
shade and protect the grass. On one long side of the lawn,
against the wall, will be planted the aromatic and medicinal
herbs: rue, sage, basil, etc. On the north end should be planted
the flowers: violets, columbine, lilies, roses, iris, and other like.
On the end where the flowers are planted the ground should be
terraced so that it will be possible to sit at ease and be reposed
in spirit. In a briefer description John of Garland, also of the
thirteenth century, limits the flowers to roses, violets, and lilies,
and adds such pot-herbs as onions, leeks, garlic, beets, melons,
and cucumbers. We learn from Crisp that the central grass
turf was very often a flowery mead—a meadow in which flowers,
domestic and wild, were encouraged to grow not too thickly. We
know also that all beds, whether they contained flowers or
herbs, were slightly raised (2 to 4 inches) with a retaining row
of bricks or a board in front.[3] In a bed of flowers grass was
encouraged to grow.

The sort of garden which Albertus Magnus had in mind
would be the kind where space was not too much at a premium

---

[1] Sir Frank Crisp, *Mediaeval Gardens* (London, 1924). 2 vols., limited
edition. Albert Forbes Sieveking, *Gardens Ancient and Modern* (London,
1899).

[2] Albertus Magnus, *De vegetabilibus libri VII*, ed. Ernst Mayer, (Ber-
lin, 1867), Bk. VII, tract. I, cap. 14.

[3] Crisp, *op. cit.*, pp. 54-57.

and where the proprietor had some interest in medicine and aromatic spices.   There is a smaller garden, however, which is mentioned by the poets, where shade, cooling water, and a flowery mead were all that was desired.   Such a place is described in the *Cligés* of Chrétien de Troyes.   It is a castle garden attached to the donjon, and undoubtedly inside the curtain wall which surrounded the courtyard.

> "Through the little door did she enter into the garden which pleased her much, and suited her. In the very center was a fruit tree loaded with blossoms and with some leaves, and this tree was broad at the top. The branches were so trained that they pointed toward the ground and reached low, except those on the crown of the tree. The crown extended straight upward. Underneath the tree was a very delightful and lovely meadow; never could the sun climb so high at mid-day when it is hottest that the rays would pass through. Jehan knew so well how to arrange and train the branches. Fenice was wont to go there to take delight, and she made her couch there. The garden was closed all around by a high wall which extended to the castle tower, so that no one could enter if he did not pass through the tower itself."[4]

In the *Lanval* of Marie de France, after the Feast of St. John thirty knights take their ease in a garden which is directly below the donjon where Queen Guenevere is in residence.   She sees them from her window and descends the steps with thirty of her maidens, going directly into the garden.[5]   Obviously this attractive spot must have been entered from the donjon.   Chrétien de Troyes had a fondness for gardens.   In the *Yvain* Calogrenanz and the daughter of the *vavassor* go into a garden with a pleasant little meadow, surrounded by a low wall, from the courtyard of the castle.[6]   Also in the *Yvain* the protagonist stops at the Castle of Pesme Aventure.   Within the court or *baillie*, to which he is introduced by the porter, there is the donjon and in addition a *grant salle* which is *haute et neuve*.   This *salle* was a separate building.   Yvain goes through this *salle* or *meison* into a garden lying within the curtain wall of the castle.   It is there that he finds the lord and lady and their daughter reclining on the turf while the daughter reads from a romance.[7]   In this same courtyard there is another enclosure directly in front of the *grant salle*.   It is a meadow surrounded by high pales—round and

---

4 *Cligés*, vv. 6402-24.
5 *Lanval*, vv. 225, 247-50.
6 *Yvain*, vv. 238-40.
7 *Ibid.*, vv. 5191 ff.

sharpened at the tips—in which girls are kept who do handiwork under "sweatshop" conditions.[8]

A central tree with its heavy shade was often a basic requirement for the less formal garden. Although more than one tree is mentioned in the Spanish *Razón de Amor*, the ingredients are similar:

> In the month of April, after dining, I stood under an olive tree among the trees of a garden. I saw too pitchers, one of silver filled with a fine red wine, covered so that the heat might not touch it; the other was full of cold water which bubbled up in that garden. I laid my head on a bit of turf and removed my clothing so that I might not suffer from the heat. Later I went to the perennial spring—never did one see such a fountain anywhere. It had such power that due to its coolness you did not feel the heat for a hundred paces around. All sorts of sweet smelling herbs were near that spring. There was salvia, roses, lilies, violets; there were so many plants that I could not name them all. But the sweet that came from them would raise a man from the dead . . .[9]

It is entirely possible, as D. W. Robertson has intimated, that gardens thus described in lyrics and romances can be interpreted on a higher level than the literal.[10] However, the descriptions are not imaginary on the literal level, and must have had a resemblance to the actual gardens of the twelfth and thirteenth centuries. Obviously a garden of that time was an outdoor living room, with coolness provided by the shade tree and running water. The grass made a delightfully soft couch and from the flowers and herbs there flowed fragrant odors.

In the *De honeste amandi* of Andreas Capellanus there is a garden which is undoubtedly symbolical; but its plan does not seem impossible for a real garden. It was arranged in three concentric circles. In the very center was a "marvellously tall tree, bearing abundantly all sorts of fruit, with its branches extending as far as the very edge of this innermost division. At the roots of this tree there gushed forth a wonderful spring of the clearest water, which to those who drank it tasted like the sweetest nectar. . . ."[11]

In the *Roman de la Rose* is the most famous garden of them all.[12] If this had existed in reality it would have been much

---

[8] *Ibid.*, vv. 5349-408.
[9] *The Oxford Book of Spanish Verse*, p. 1. This is thirteenth century.
[10] D. W. Robertson in *Speculum* XXVI (1951), 24-49. Also one is reminded of the description of the Garden of Eden. Genesis 2:9-10.
[11] *The Art of Courtly Love*, tr. J. J. Parry (New York, 1941), pp. 78-79.
[12] *Roman de la Rose*, vv. 516 ff.; 714-16; 1323-74.

larger than the one described by Albertus Magnus. It is clear
from what the Poet says that the section devoted to fruit trees
was set apart, as these trees were planted at regular intervals
of thirty feet. This large garden was surrounded by a high wall
and the Poet had difficulty finding an entrance. Once inside he
saw a verdure beautiful beyond all belief. There was a path,
lined with sweet fennel and mint, which he followed towards the
central green sward where dancing was in progress. After brief
participation in this amusement the Poet explored further. He
saw lovely laurel trees, pines, cedars, mulberries. There was no
fruit tree that was not there—apple trees, pomegranates, muscat
nut trees, almond trees, fig trees, and dates. Among the more
exotic aromatic plants were cloves, liquorice, Malagueta pepper,
zedoary, and cinnamon, which, to be sure, do not grow in any
garden in France. This was a touch from the East. There was
also dill, which is found in France. In addition the Poet saw
olives and cypress, which, he assures us, are rarely grown in
France. Then there were elms, big and branchy, and beeches,
and hornbeams,[13] as well as straight hazel trees, aspens, and the
ash. The branches of all these are described as so long and high
that they made a perpetual shade and protection from the sun.
In further description Guillaume de Lorris mentions that there
were streams which made a pleasant, lovely ripple as they flowed
in the shade, with basins or pools around which the grass grew
as was suitable. In this moist grass were violets and peri-
winkle. The green sward was dotted with white, red, and yellow
flowers—a flowering mead. The garden also had quinces,
peaches, chestnuts, other nut trees, pears, medlars, black and
white plums, cherries, sorb apples, and loteberry trees. It would
be useless to attempt to divine the precise layout of this garden
but with Albertus Magnus by our side we may guess the general
arrangement. There was a large central grassy area which was
protected by thick shade trees. The orchard would be at one
extremity, perhaps divided off by a lattice rail fence with a
central gateway. The herbs were doubtless set out around the
wall, some in raised beds. The flowers were growing here and
there in the grass, especially beside the streams and pools.

We turn now to some speculation about the royal garden of
the city of Paris. As many of my readers know, the city was

---

[13] The hornbeam or *charme* (<*carpinu*) was associated with love and
beauty because of its homonimity with *charme* (<*carmina*). The *Roman
de la Rose*, v. 524, speaks of "Le guichet, qui estoit de charme."

originally concentrated on a long island, resembling somewhat a ship, which lay in the Seine river. There were six other smaller islands strung out at both ends of the Cité, but these were not to be occupied for many generations to come. At the "bow" or western tip of the great Isle de la Cité was the King's royal enclosure. Around the whole island, set back a bit from the steep bank at the water's edge, was the old crumbling ruin of a Roman wall. This wall had a walk along the top but no defense towers. There is a representation of this royal enclosure, dating from around 1415, in the *Tresriches Heures* of the Duc de Berry for the month of June.[14] The view was painted from his own town house, the Chasteau de Nesle, just across the Seine. Proportions are not very good; the river is made too narrow. The buildings shown are those of Philip IVth, the Fair, at the very close of the thirteenth century. We assume that in the twelfth and thirteenth centuries there were two principal buildings, the donjon in which the king lived with his family, and the *grant salle* or vast audience hall, which may have been of Merovingian (possibly Roman) construction. This *salle* was celebrated. Leading to the entrance courtyard were broad steps up which knights could—on occasion—ride their horses. The back windows of this *salle* faced onto the royal garden, which filled the extreme tip of the island. In the *Tresriches Heures* we see the near wall lined with espaliers on which trees and vines are trained. We have no description of this garden, but Alexander Neckam, during his residence in Paris, gave specifications for the planting of a rich garden, and we will assume for the sake of convenience that he had the royal garden in mind.[15]

Alexander says of such a garden that it should be ornamented with lilies, roses, heliotropes, violets, and mandrakes; also with sweet Mary (Chrysanthemum Balsamita), fennel, southernwood, coriander, sage, savory, hyssop, mint, rue, dittany, celery, pyrethrum, lettuce, cress, and peonies. There should also be beds of onions, leeks, garlic, pumpkins, and shallots. Alexander continues and includes cucumbers, poppies, daffodils, and acanthus, which, he says, are to be seen in "distinguished" gardens. Other good things he lists as beets, fool's parsley, orach or mountain spinach, sorrel, and mallows—which he calls pot-herbs. For giving usefulness Alexander then names anise,

---

[14] These illuminations are reproduced in *Life*, XXIV (January 5, 1948), 38-50.
[15] *De naturis rerum*, ed. Thomas Wright (London, 1863), pp. 274-75.

mustard, white pepper, and absinthe. Next he comes to the trees of a "noble garden," namely medlars, quinces, winter pears. St. Regulus pears, peaches, pomegranates, lemons, oranges, dates, and figs. (These would suggest that Alexander had in mind a Spanish garden rather than one in the Paris region.) He is by no means through at this point, although he is careful to note that the following did not grow in Europe at all: ginger, clove, cinnamon, liquorice, zedoary root, incense, myrrh, aloes, oil of myrrh, rosin, storax, balsam, galbanum, nard, Arabian oil of myrrh, and cassia fistula. He mentions cypress, too. Then he includes certain medicinal herbs which do grow in France, as he remarks: saffron, sandyx, thyme, pennyroyal, borage, purselain, and wild spikenard. He mentions colewort and ragwort, which excite love, and psyllium, of which the marvellous frigidity offers a remedy for that affliction. Myrtle is listed as a friend of temperance. The author concludes this catalogue with hound's tongue and bryony.

The layout of a planting as complicated as all this (omitting the exotic "noble" trees and the Oriental spices and balsams) might be similar to what we imagined for the garden in the *Roman de la Rose*. Anyone who owned a garden so sumptuous would not have used vegetables as basic foods. Many vegetables were considered medicinal and they were employed also for the flavoring of meat dishes. In a *Miracle* of Gautier de Councy (thirteenth century) there is mention of "poree au mouton" as a fine dish alongside of fish and meat. Within a few lines it is contrasted with meager cloister fare of "poree en lainges" and "pois au jus." The first is lamb stew flavored with beets; the others are beets in their skins and peas in their own juice.[16] In the *Hortulus* of Walahfrid Strabo of St. Gall there is a magnificent list of twenty-three herbs and vegetables cultivated in the ninth century garden of St. Gall.[17] This, of course, provided cloister fare and medicine. The herbs are sage, cucumbers, absinthe, hoarhound, fennel, gladiola, chervil, lilies, poppies, mint, celery, bettony, turnip, roses—and the following which I will cite in the Latin form given: *ruta, abrotonum, cucurbita, libisticum, sclarea, puleum, agrimonia, ambrosia, nepeta,* and *raphanus.* Some of these are better known to us as flowering plants; but that is hardly why they were planted in the garden at St. Gall.

---

[16] *De la bonne empereriz qui garda loiaument sen mariage,* ed. Erik von Kraemer (Helsinki, 1953), vv. 2944, 3648.

[17] Migne, *P.L.,* 114, cols. 1120-30.

Eginhard has preserved for posterity the plan of the St. Gall garden.[18] The herbs are in eighteen rectangular (raised?) beds, forming two "columns" of nine beds each. Adjacent to this walled herb garden, but not attached to it, is the cemetery which serves also as an orchard. Fruit trees grow between the graves and against the wall. Such a cemetery is depicted in Chrétien's *Cligés*. Indeed, the protagonist gains entrance into a locked cemetery by climbing into a fruit tree which leans over the wall.[19] A garden or orchard consisting only of trees was possible "Before the gate (of the castle) is a garden which consists of diverse trees."[20]

It is remarkable how the arrangement of a tall shade tree with a fountain or stream flowing coolly beside it seemed ideal even where there was no formal garden. In the *Yvain* of Chrétien this is the grouping at the Magic Fountain, which may well have been in the midst of a wood, judging from the isolation described and the number of trees near-by. In the *Girart de Roussillon* there is a more unusual arrangement. At Saint-Eloi Charles Martel held council with his barons. Between the curtain wall and the palace there was an attractive level place where stone seats were skillfully placed with cement. These were ornamented with bestiary designs in mosaic of resplendent gold. The pavement was of bright *marevitre* (?). In the central position was a pine tree which protected against the heat. Around it stirred a breeze which smelled sweeter than incense or spiced wine. A fountain was fed from a slope, the water spouting forth from a golden stag's head. Entry into this charming place was forbidden to people of lower social condition.[21] Turf, flowers, and plants were missing, but it served much the same purpose as an outdoor garden. One might think that the southern Frenchman who wrote the *Girart de Roussillon* had crossed in his mind the concept of the garden with the ruins of a Roman amphitheater. We doubt that a place like this existed.

The *Lai de l'Oiselet* portrays the garden of a manor house where the garden is oblong in shape (*lons . . . a conpas roons*) but enclosed only by trees and a running stream. Despite this informality it contains herbs, flowers, and spices of delicious

---

[18] Crisp, pp. 54-57; figure CCXXIII.
[19] *Cligés*, vv. 6194-99.
[20] *Le jongleur Gautier le Leu*, ed. C. H. Livingston (Cambridge, Mass., 1951), vv. 232-33, p. 245.
[21] *Girart de Roussillon*, ed. W. Mary Hackett (Paris, 1953), vv. 2136-46.

odor, and has the fountain in the center shaded by a tall pine tree.[21a]

In the descriptions given thus far, special mention is made of running water, pools, and fountains, which were considered very necessary for cooling the pleasant air. For many years the present writer was doubtful of the existence of actual stone fountains as early as the twelfth and thirteenth centuries, unless some persisted from ancient gardens, but there are several excellent examples in the mediaeval room of the Philadelphia Museum of Art. The one from Saint-Michel de Cuxa obviously operated only when its box-like reservoir was filled with water (by hand buckets?) and this must have been for special occasions only. In fifteenth century garden miniatures, ornate fountains of this kind can frequently be seen, although the method of operating them is even less obvious.

Wild flowers were doubtless encouraged to grow in the central grass turf, or flowery mead, but they are almost invariably omitted from descriptions. Perhaps they did not give that elegant touch which the mediaeval man sought to create. Wild flowers grow more profusely in western Europe than they do in the United States. They are likely to be bigger, too, with larger leaves in the northern climes.[22] The ox-eye daisy and the buttercup are choice examples of this profusion. The foxglove, the corn-poppy, the speedwell or veronica, the wild hyacinth, the primrose, the different vetches, and the forget-me-nots are very plentiful there in the proper season. The little daisy, "the wee modest crimson-tippit flow'r," is nearly as universal as is grass. When Nicolette was walking in the meadow outside Beaucaire, she had toes so white that the daisies looked outright black in comparison.[23]

The rose was the most highly prized of domestic flowers, and it was valued also for its curative effects on stomach, liver, kidneys, skin, and other parts. For medicine it was prepared as rose honey, sugared rose, sirop, oil of rose, and rose water.[24] There were probably three basic domestic varieties cultivated at this time in Europe: the cabbage rose, the Provins rose, and the

---

[21a] *Medieval Studies in memory of Gertrude Schoepperle Loomis* (Paris; New York, 1927), pp. 343-44.

[22] John Burroughs, *Fresh Fields* (Edinburgh, 1909), Ch. VIII. "A Glance at British Wildflowers."

[23] *Aucassin et Nicolette*, section XII.

[24] Charles Joret, *La rose dans l'antiquité et au moyen âge* (Paris, 1892), pp. 466 ff.

damask rose.[25] There were three wild varieties also: the dog rose, the sweetbrier, and the common field rose. According to Mat-thiolus there were three colors: pink (*incarnato*), red (*russo*) and white.[26] The *Roman de la Rose* gives a description:

> When I had approached the rose I found it grown a little large, and I saw that it had increased since I last saw it close to hand; it was not yet sufficiently opened so that the seeds could be seen—they were still enclosed within the petals of the rose which were standing erect *and filling all the space inside the flower*. The seeds did not appear, so full was the rose. It was, thanks to God, more advanced than it had been and was still more red.[27]

This was certainly a beautiful cabbage rose. From the *Roman de la Rose* we should judge that roses could be planted apart in a rose garden surrounded by high hedges.[28]

Lilies also were popular. Matthiolus illustrates varieties which appear to be the Easter lily, the orange lily, and the narcissus as we know them. The violet which he describes must have been our familiar variety. He says that it could be either purple or yellow and that it had leaves resembling the ivy, al-though smaller.

It is claimed that the *fleur de lis* decoration so often met with in French heraldry goes back to ornamentation on the points of the royal crown, and that this was copied from the Byzantines. It is also stated that the flower imitated for this was the iris, more properly the variety which we know as Dutch or Siberian iris. Dead white coloring is basic with that variety. In the *Roman de la Rose* a lady is "simple as a bride, with flesh tender as dew and as white as the *flor de lis*."[29]

Flowers were picked or cut for various purposes. Young women, and sometimes young men, wore chaplets of blossoms around their hair. In a certain carving of the labors of the twelve months dating from the twelfth century, there is for the month of April the figure of a young man with such a band of flowers around his head. Some art historians have thought that a woman was intended![30] A cut flower might be carried in the

---

[25] *Ibid.*, pp. 166-68.
[26] *I Discorsi di M. Pietro Andrea Matthioli* (Venice, 1585), pp. 202-4. Matthioli says (p. 204) there is a yellow variety which is ill smelling. Surely that could not be a true rose!
[34] *Laustic*, vv. 95-100.
[27] *Roman de la Rose*, vv. 3357-70.
[28] *Ibid.*, vv. 2779-80.
[29] *Ibid.*, v. 1001.
[30] James Carson Webster, *The Labors of the Months* (Evanston, Illinois, 1938).

hand. In the winter, dried grasses and rushes were scattered on the floors of tile or brick inside houses; in spring and summer green grass and flowers were used instead. It was customary for people to sit on the floors, especially when a large gathering was present. They got the full benefit of pleasant odors as well as of the bad. Sweet-smelling balsam would be placed in calabashes or gourds and these would be hung in the open window frames of houses. The spring breezes would waft into a room this delicious smell, which was apt to surpass in sweetness what was present directly outside.

A mediaeval garden is seldom well described without mention of the birds. Guillaume de Lorris knew many and was probably aware of their potentialities as singers, judging from the order in which he lists them.[31] In one spot, he says, were the nightingales, in another jays and starlings. There were also great flocks of gold crests and turtledoves, of goldfinches, of swallows, of larks, of *lardereles* (titmice?). The calendar larks were grouped in another place, and they were never tired of singing. There were blackbirds and song thrushes, which yearned to compete with the other birds in song. There were popinjays, and still other birds throughout the groves.

Such a concentration would hardly be found anywhere, even when we consider the better conditions for wild life in the Middle Ages. This listing became commonplace in later literature, imitated from the *Roman de la Rose*. We will accept it at its face value. The nightingale was and is the most noble of all birds. It is a spectacular as well as a sweet singer. Mentioned throughout all literature, it received its first adequate eulogy from Pliny.[32] A German observer of today once tried to record in words the variety of its song. We repeat about a third of this:

> Tiou o, tiou o, tiou o, tiou o—Shpe tiou tokoua—tio tio tio— kouotio kouotio kouotio kouotio—tskouo tskouo tskouo tskouo, tsiitsiitsiitsiitsiitsiitsiitsiit—kouoror tiou—tskous pipitskouisi— tsotsotsotsotsotsotsotsotsotso tsrrhading—tsisis si toso si si si si si si si—tsorre, tsorre, tsorre, tsorrehitsantsantsantsantsant- santsantsi—dlo,dlo,dla,dla,dlodlodlodlodlo—kouio trrrrrrrrrritzt— lu,lu,lu,ly,ly,ly,li,li,li . . . . . . higuai,guai,guay guaiguaiguaiguai- guai—kouior tsio siopi.[33]

[31] *Roman de la Rose*, vv. 644-60. St. Bernard of Clairvaux says that a garden should have water, varied trees, varied grasses, and a concert of many colored birds. Sieveking, *op. cit.*, pp. 32-33.

[32] X, 63.

[33] The transcription is by Bechstein. See Salvador Novo, *Las aves en la poesia castellana* (Mexico City, 1953), p. 17.

This sequence of trills and churrs only approximates the lovely descending chromatic tones of this demure brown thrush, which has always expressed so adequately the sadness of love for countless generations of humans; but it will help those who have no idea of the nightingale's song. In the *Laustic* of Marie de France a lady and her lover live in adjacent donjons, with a single wall between the two premises. They can be aware of each other when they stand at the window. They are accustomed to doing this while listening to the nightingale every night. The husband of the lady traps the little bird and wrings its neck.[34] Probably the bird was nesting in the husband's garden since he had it caught so easily.

It is not without reason that the nightingale is followed by the jay and the starling, although this might appear odd to an American reader, who has other ideas about those two birds. The European jay (browner than our bluejay) is famed for its imitation of animals and other birds; the starling has a series of extremely varied notes, imitating successfully many sounds: whistling, coughing, kissing, chuckling, and even wheezing. The mediaeval listener appreciated these two as among the best vocal artists of Nature. The birds in the list which come next are known for their mating dances. The *roitelet* or gold crest has such a dance, in which it hovers long in the air while chirping. The turtledove is much larger by far, but it also is a perfect lover, bobbing up and down in rapid succession while courting. The goldfinch offers a nuptial display of wings. If I am correct in assuming that these three birds were listed because of these habits, then we must accept Guillaume de Lorris as no mean observer. With the swallow we return to characteristics of song. This common black and white flier has a markedly lively, cheery twittering which is delivered both on the wing and while perching. The skylark is famed for its beautiful notes uttered as it soars up on high, almost vertically, for as much as a thousand feet. This is punctuated by a few pauses and then the bird changes key and glides down to the earth. I hesitate to translate *lardereles* as titmice, for the great tit, the coal tit, the marsh tit, and the blue tit do not belong in this company. They have only a slight variation of "Teach-er, teacher" for a song.

The calendar lark (Melanocorypha) is a noted singer of the south of Europe and of northern Africa. It is the largest of

---

[34] *Laustic*, vv. 95-10.0

the larks, being some eight inches and more in length. Its
coloration is marked by brown on the top of the head and black
on the throat, but it has whitish underparts and white on the
secondary wing feathers. It is a favorite bird in the bestiaries
where it is assumed to have special power on the couch of dying
individuals. This *calandría* is quite common on the Castilian
plateau during the summer months where it is often captured
and caged. While in captivity the bird becomes an excellent
mimic of other birds. The cages are always provided with a
sandy bottom and a cloth roof. The *calandría,* being a lark, is
used to flying straight up when it begins to sing and the cloth
prevents damage.

The blackbird or merle needs no introduction to the American reader of Mother Goose. Its mellow song from January to
the end of July is a feature of the European gardens and countryside. The bestiaries claim that this bird sings for three
months only, which is not accurate. The song thrush or mavis
is even a finer performer. From March to July it sings all day
long, and again in the autumn. Its most common phrase is a
melodious "Did he do it? Did he do it?" This bird also has a
courting dance.

The last in the bird list given by Guillaume de Lorris is the
popinjay or parrot. Surely the West African Grey Parrot was
the bird usually designated by that name. Of all the birds of
the Old World this is the best talker and mimic, and we have
noted that mimicry was an ability much sought after. We know
that parrots and monkeys were immensely popular as pets in
the twelfth and thirteenth centuries and later. They were im-
ported, to be sure, and the likeliest route must have been through
Spain. The Grey Parrot and the Barbary Ape are common
directly across the Straits of Gibraltar. In fact this ape, a
fawn-colored, tailless monkey, occurs on Gibraltar itself. It has
always been a favorite with organ grinders in Europe. Its tailless form is recognizable in many mediaeval representations—
notably in the charming carving of a minstrel and his monkey
on the wall of the nave arcade at Bayeux Cathedral.

After our survey of the gardens of the twelfth century
Renaissance period we are aware that the simplest form required only a large shade tree, a green turf, and a pleasant
stream. To go beyond that was to have herbs: aromatic, medicinal, and of the pot variety, with some flowers, and a few fruit

trees, laid out around a central turf. We assume that a low wall was desirable in any case. Larger gardens had many more of all these plants, and often a separate section which we would call an orchard. The stretch of green turf, dotted with many-colored flowers, and cooled and moistened by a stream with a pool or fountain, was, of course, a necessity. Fruit trees were more often than not trimmed and trained upon espaliers. If we wish to picture the possible pergolas, the lattice fences, and other appurtenances, we must turn to miniatures of gardens in the fifteenth and sixteenth centuries. I like to think that there was a minimum of these in our earlier period, and that raised plant beds and a grassy terrace near the sweet-smelling flowers and herbs were all that was required. In the most characteristic centuries of the Middle Ages men and women were content with few gadgets. They could sit on the floor or on the ground very comfortably. They did not even demand beautiful vistas; they concentrated on the immediate scene before them. Conditioned as they were to fortified castle or walled town, they learned to be content with little space, and it is small wonder that the mind's eye often turned inward upon itself.

A TWELFTH-CENTURY SCHOOLMASTER

III

A TWELFTH-CENTURY SCHOOLMASTER

IN THIS PRESENT ESSAY we seek to bring the reader to a peaceful contemplation of the daily routine of a *lector* or *clerc lisant* in the schools of Paris in the last quarter of the twelfth century. He will be the equivalent of our contemporary under-graduate teacher. We have chosen Paris because its schools were the most prominent in all of Europe and always had a considerable colony of English masters and students. All educated people in England of that date bemoaned their misfortune if they had not studied at Paris. A certain nun who wrote the life of Saint Edward the Confessor, around 1160, apologizes because her Anglo-Norman French is defective in the use of verb and noun inflexions. After all, she says, she has not had the privilege of studying on the continent.[1]

Before we find our way to the home of the schoolmaster we shall visit, we shall glance briefly at the city itself. Our earliest extant map of Paris dates from about 1530, but the first one of useful size and detail is the one prepared by Olivier Truschet and Germain Hoyau towards 1551. Not until the plan by Jacques Gomboust in 1652 do we have a map drawn to scale. This is very valuable in presenting the history of the early French theaters. The Truschet-Hoyau map is usually reproduced in sections by those who desire to illustrate the career of François Villon and other fifteenth century characters. There is nothing to give us the mediaeval picture of the great city except the undetailed drawing prepared by M. Halphen, and a slightly more detailed sketch which I have presented by combining Halphen, the streets to scale from the Gomboust, and the information on streets and buildings drawn from cartularies and other twelfth century sources. This last is the city such as I shall now describe it, as it could have been in 1175-89.[2]

There was a stockade of some kind on the right bank. Probably this was made with huge wooden pales, sharpened at the top. The two or three gateways leading into this suburban en-

---

[1] *La vie d'Edouard le confesseur*, ed. Södergard (Uppsala, 1949), vv 1 ff.

[2] The material on mediaeval Paris and daily life in the Middle Ages which now follows in this essay is founded on many sources, which are indicated in my *Daily Living in the Twelfth Century* (The University of Wisconsin Press, 1952, 1953). The map of Paris is printed as an end-sheet in this book.

closure were of stone. We are sure of two of these gates, the Porte Baudoyer and the Porte Saint-Merri, but we are not informed positively on the existence of a gate at the western end, or on its position with respect to the Chastelet through which one entered the Pont aux changes. The Chastelet itself was usually called the Porte de Paris. Travellers approaching the city from Italy and Provence, as well as those coming from north and east, were accustomed to entering the Isle de la Cité from this right bank. The Grant Rue of the left bank, which began at the Petit Chastelet or entrance to the Petit Pont, was very definitely the Orleans Road. It is understood that the Isle, which resembled a ship in general shape, was the main area of the city of Paris. It was still enclosed by an old wall of the Roman period which had no towers and which stood some yards back from the edge of the water. The right bank stockade included a broad open space which ran to the very edge of the water. This was the Grève. Earlier in the century it had been the principal market of Paris, but now this was outside the Porte de Paris and the Grève had become the Wine Market. Ships were floated down the Seine loaded with casks of wine which had been transferred from barges on the Saone River, coming from Burgundy and Lorraine. These were tied up at the Grève. The wealthiest merchants of the city had their town houses facing on this open space with its freer circulation of air, an air laden with the perfume of fine spiced wines. The Porte Baudoyer which received travellers from the East and from Italy was most important. There was a hospice there maintained by the church of Saint-Gervais. At the very close of the century the church of Sainte-Opportune near the Porte de Paris opened another hospice for travellers who came from the north, down the Chaussee Saint-Denis. All the roads and streets were muddy—a peculiarly black mud—except where there were remnants of Roman paving: on the Rue Saint-Martin, the Rue des Juifs, the Rue du Petit Pont, and on the Orleans Road (left bank). These had formed a continuous Roman highway before the Roman bridge across the Seine had fallen down. In 1185 there was to be made a new start towards paving the main streets in the city proper.

Our visit to the schoolmaster will take place in the closing years of the reign of King Louis VII, who died in 1180. At this date the Rue de la Juiverie was still there, famous for its bakeshops. A long street leading from there to the Rue devant le Palais du Roi was that of the Drapers, which was lined by the shops of some of the wealthiest tradesmen in the city. The royal palace consisted chiefly of an audience hall, built in the Merovingian era, and a donjon or protected tower in which the king had his private apartments. There was a royal garden at the western tip of the island, within this enclosure. By 1180 the choir of the new Church of Notre Dame had been completed, but the Bishop's cathedral was still the Merovingian Church of the Blessed Mary which was located slightly to the front of Notre Dame. A new street, the Rue Neuve Notre Dame, had been opened in 1163 to permit easy circulation of traffic from the cathedral to the Petit Pont.

Students were now forbidden to lodge within the cloister of the cathedral, and classes could no longer be held there. This edict dated from 1127. Consequently the maze of little streets between the cathedral and the Rue de la Juiverie contained the majority of the student lodgings, and many of the masters' houses where classes were taught were also scattered about in this space. One or two of the masters were teaching on the Petit Pont itself, which was a better summer than winter location. The Pont had open spaces with stone seats between several of its houses, and it was possible to gaze from these down upon the flowing water. Perhaps some classes were even held in those openings during the warmer months. The usual place for a class was in the *rez de chaussée* of a master's house. This room, which filled the entire street floor, was normally intended for a shop at the front of a burgher's house. In winter rushes, and in summer greener things, were strewn upon the floor. The scholars sat among the rushes or on an occasional bench while the *lector* occupied a chair which may have had a writing stand before it. Some listeners, if the master were popular, must have stood out in the street, catching what they could over the drone and bellowing from passers-by.

The left bank of the Seine was a hill, covered rather plentifully with vineyards marked off by hedgerows into sections or *clos*. The Orleans road led straight up the hill and disappeared at the top into the distance. On the hill top to the left of the road the abbey of Sainte-Geneviève was conspicuous, with a few crowded streets in front of it. Otherwise this distant left bank view was peaceful and bucolic—or perhaps, Bacchic. The abbots of Sainte-Genevieve, Saint-Victor, and Saint-Germain-des-prés, as well as the Cathedral chapter, were very slow in encouraging building on these lands. Only down by the river, and immediately around the entrance of Petit Pont, were dwellings in evidence at this time. There was a long street which parallelled the river. On the left side of the Orleans Road it was the Rue de la Boucherie; on the right it became Rue de la Huchette. The houses of masters and student boarding houses were very frequent along this street, sprinkled among the stalls of wood merchants, butchers, and fish dealers. There was no lack of provender here. A church had been newly built for this suburb; it was the Church of Saint-Julien and this was much in demand by the students and masters as a place for holding disputations and defense of theses. There was another new church, Saint-Severin, across the Orleans Road.

Having given our readers a brief guided tour through the lovely city of Paris we must now select a protagonist among the *lectores* or *clers lisanz*. We will choose a typical, ordinary individual, not a teacher of great distinction, and we will assume that his house was on the Rue de la Boucherie. From a small window in the rear he was able to gaze across the Seine to the construction which was in progress on the new Cathedral of Notre Dame. The two ornamental windows with rounded arches looking out at the front from the *premier étage* gave a view of the muddy little street, which carried traffic from the Petit Pont area to the monastery of Saint-Victor. Like all properly laid mediaeval streets, this road had an open drain down the center which eventually emptied its refuse into the new channel of the Bièvre, which had recently been dug by the Victorine canons. This kind of open drain served a very useful purpose in a climate with much rainfall, like that of Paris, but our *lector* did not have much concern for it, because the river was at the back of his house and it made a more effective sewer. (The Seine had a swifter current than it does now. Since the nineteenth century these tidal rivers have been slowed down by dams or weirs. By the same token the river was shallower than it is now.)

The *lector* whom we have selected will be called Guillaume, or rather Mestre Guillaume, to allow him his professional title. Since his name was a very common one it was more accurate to refer to him as Mestre Guillaume de Mucegros, attaching to his name the small hamlet from which he came, in the French

Vexin, west of Paris. His father, who had been a serf, was Gilbert Bouche, and Guillaume did not wish to be known among his peers as Willelmus Bucca. Guillaume was a teacher of the Trivium—Grammar, Rhetoric, and Dialectic—and nearly all his students were young in years, probably twelve to fifteen years old. Farther up the hill from his house was a straw market which was not yet a street, but which was destined to be called the Rue de la Paille and to be a popular location for teachers of the Trivium.

Mestre Guillaume was in lower orders of the Church, so he affected black clothing, or at least dress of a dark hue. He had been obliged to renounce all hope of more advanced teaching some years before when he married. At the time that we are observing his activity there were six mouths to feed in his household: himself, his wife, a son and a daughter, an upstairs maid who was also a relation from Mucegros, and a boy of all work who was no relation at all, for which they were glad.

Guillaume and his family lived on the *premier étage* of their house. Their principal room was the second-floor front, in our parlance. The floor was of brick, and the same could be said of the fireplace. The walls, however, were perpendicular boards, rough hewn on the inside. This interior wall was covered completely by a set of hangings which were strung around the entire room. They were of heavy linen, dyed green, and were substantial enough to keep out cold and damp. The ceiling beams were visible, painted blue and red with a paint that had a mixed linseed and turpentine base. All of this would have made a beautiful fire if someone should be careless with a hot coal or a candle. Mestre Guillaume and his wife, and perhaps the others also, were unusually careful about this. The teacher had invested his all in this house, which enabled him to earn his living. He used a tall floor candle stick with a sharp prong at its top. This stood well out into the middle of the floor. There was a screen covered with green parchment which could be placed against the double window of this room if the weather demanded it. When it was in place the room was considerably darker, but the inhabitants did not demand much light except from the candle and the fireplace.

The furnishings consisted of one large chair with back and arm rests, which stood close to the fire, a few benches and stools (with very low backs) which were placed against the hangings, several massive wooden chests, and a bed which was covered with a red mattress pad. This bed was not dismantled because it served as a soft couch for the lady of the household during the day. Other beds, disassembled, were standing behind the hangings, close to the wooden wall, and there was a wooden table top there also together with two trestles on which it could be set. This table was brought out twice a day for the two meals— *vers Sexte* and at *Vespre,* or, in the language of the clock of later centuries, at eleven thirty and at six in the evening. When the table was covered with its long white cloth Mestre Guillaume sat at one side of it in the tall armchair with his back to the fire. The others, except for the serving boy, placed themselves on benches to his right and left. The boy fetched up the food from the kitchen below.

There was an inner room, or closet, on this floor, at the rear of the house. This was entered from the main room just described. Here there was only one small window, rather high up, and the walls were not completely covered with hangings. On one wooden wall there was a long pole supported by two brackets, about five feet above the brick floor. On this clothing was draped. All sorts of household gear were stowed in this smaller room, although it had a few dismantled beds and could serve as a sleeping room too. In other houses this chamber might have had a chute or drop descending to the garderobe pit in the kitchen, which was below ground level. The seat for this toilet chute would have been cut into a ledge along the wall. Guillaume had never yielded to the temptation to do this because he did not think it necessary, and it would have been unsightly to have this chute passing through the *aula* or classroom, which made up the entire ground floor of the house.

The family bath tub was in this closet or inner room. It looked more like a modern beer keg than anything else. It was large enough to have a small three-legged stool placed inside on which the bather could sit by the hour until his hot water grew too cold for comfort. When not in use this tub was kept bottom up; it was then a convenient ledge for laying things on, and also served as a table. Clothing and leather objects flung there were out of the way of the mice. The source for the hot water was the kitchen fire, which was two stories down. Six pots of the steaming fluid had to be carried upstairs, along with an equal amount of cold. It may be asked why they did not use the fireplace in the main room. Water had to be brought up anyway from the ground level, and could be carried just as easily after it had been heated. Muscles were not so stiff then as they are now, and it was not thought inconvenient to run up and down several flights of stairs. It was rare for an individual to bathe once a day, but it was not unknown. Some preferred to enter the tub just four times a year, after each of the seasonal blood-lettings. On such occasions the patient would lie in bed quietly for a day or so after the *mire* had drawn the blood into a basin. On rising, the new-made man would celebrate by getting immediately into his bath. If the family could afford two bath tubs, it was most pleasant to bathe in company. The man might wear his close fitting snood cap, to keep from getting a chill. Probably the serving boy took his baths in a less elegant container, somewhere in the kitchen, where he had to fetch very little water.

There was a third floor at the top of the house. It was the *soler,* a single room under the roof. This particular apartment was rented to several students who kept house there. Mestre Guillaume's boy was called upon to bring things to them for a little extra money. Sometimes they were displeased with him and threatened to hire another servitor of their own.

By this time the reader must be curious about the kitchen. But first we should speak of the stairway. This was in a little tower of brick and stone which stood against the interior wall of the house. Some houses had this stair tower against the outside wall, but Mestre Guillaume's abode was very close to its neighbor and the stair tower had to be inside. Inside this little tower there was a winding stone stair, cork-screw style, with a landing at each floor and a door opening into the room. At night the door on the ground level was kept well bolted, as the *aula* or classroom could not be properly shut off from the street. The stair descended to an underground level where the kitchen was located.

Like many of her contemporaries, the schoolmaster's wife would have preferred a kitchen at the back, on the ground level, but the space was needed for her husband's classes. In the dark little hole of a kitchen below stairs, with a single high ventilating window at the very top, the *lector's* wife supervised the larder. There was a good-sized open fireplace for cooking. We did not list a cook maid because help as low down the social scale as this was not very permanent, but Dame Emmeline had some assistance most of the time. She wished to do the cooking herself, and the boy was there to carry up the dishes. However, she liked to eat with her husband and children, and it was the cook maid who ladled out the pottage and removed the meat from the fire in the absence of her mistress. There were three or four pots in use: one for boiling beans and peas, one for other vegetables, and another for stewing meat. There were spits that could be turned before the fire. These were removable so that the meat could be carried up on them. The kitchen floor was bare earth, innocent of brick or tile, but it was quite dry and warm from the fire. There was a large wood block, waist-high, on which vegetables were sliced, and there was a cupboard of wooden shelves on which jams, and jars containing wines, were stored. A stone ledge at the wall near the kitchen fire contained a hole which Emmeline preferred to cover with a wooden top. Some of the neighbors were not so finicky. This was the garde-robe pit which was handy for kitchen waste and other slops. Filth from above stairs was carried down to this, and ever so often a man was sent for whose duty it was to empty out this hole. He carried the refuse up the stone stair and out the front in bucket loads where he pitched it into his cart.

There was a rickety stair from the back of the kitchen up to ground level, but this led only to a small enclosed patch of land, surrounded by wooden pales (sharp at the top) which formed the kitchen court. The Seine, which passed within a few yards, was shut away from view, but the court protected the wicker crates of chickens and other fowl, and the occasional sheep which was tethered there to be slaughtered by the boy. There was a *vivarium* or fish basin which, in the absence of modern refrigeration, kept fish fresh and unspoiled. The fish made no noise but the chickens and the geese were very vocal. However, the neighbors did not complain because they had similar yards adjacent and there was noise enough in the streets. Squawks were heard on all sides and they were a sign of prosperity. In the kitchen was a *tine* or large wooden vat, which held fresh water. Each morning this was filled by a water carrier who had a yoke placed across the back of his neck and a bucket dangling on a hook at each end of the yoke. The water was from the Seine, collected farther upstream. Emmeline used it and even drank it without ill effect, but some of the students who were newly come would take such a drink (on some rare occasion) and would be afflicted with dysentery. The regular members of the household were accustomed to the water and experienced no ill effects. They sneered at people farther up the hill on the left bank who had wells in their enclosures. Such well water was brackish. On special occasions the boy went out to buy wine at a near-by tavern and pepper and cummin spice from the apothecary. The wine was brought back in a skin, and the spices were fetched in a small parchment bag kept for such a purpose.

We have followed in some detail the household set-up of Mestre Guillaume and his good wife; now we should like to say something of their dress. The master kept his hair fairly short and had a small round tonsure at the top of his head—a simple tonsure. As we have said, his outer garment was black, or dark in hue, with wide open sleeves, and extended below the knees. His stockings were black wool or linen and they had a garter band above the knee. The shoes were of soft undyed leather. They were not good for bad weather, so the master also had pattens with wood at heel and toe. Underneath the *bliaut* or *cote* he wore the customary *braies* or loose underdrawers which every member of the male sex wore. Not strictly necessary, but as the sign of a well dressed gentleman, Guillaume usually put on a *chemise* with close fitting sleeves which were visible at the wrists. He had a leather belt around his waist. Emmeline wore a long chemise and over this, in the house, she affected a fur-lined *pellice*, with the fur, as usual, against the body. The *chemise* had long sleeves, but the *pellice* had none. When she wished to be better dressed in public the *lector's* wife wore a long *cote*, or *bliaut*, reaching to the floor, with wide open sleeves that had points that dropped towards the floor, and the upper part of her *cote* and *chemise* were slit from armpits to waist and laced quite tightly. She wore a cloth belt that went twice around the waist and tied in front. Her hair, like that of all contemporary women, was parted in the middle into two long plaits. To lend dignity to her person she preferred to appear in the guimple which she draped over her head and held in place with a band.

The *pellice* was a welcome garment in the cold indoors, especially as the climate of the Paris area was in general becoming more brisk around 1200. Western Europe was beginning to feel the effects of the approaching cold cycle which was to reach its height in 1433. Around 1430, we know from miniatures, snow on the ground was common and we learn from other sources that wolves roamed the streets of Paris at night. In the late twelfth century the cycle had two hundred more years ahead before its maximum but Mestre Guillaume often complained that it was colder than it had been when he was a boy.

Let us step for a few minutes to the front of the master's house and gaze up and down his street. Young men and boys in the clerical dress of students were pushing their way on every side. They were inclined to engage in pranks. The right of way was not very wide, and was a track of mud or of dust, according to the state of the weather. There was, to be sure, the drainage ditch that ran down through the center. From dawn till dusk there were street cries of all sorts. The most welcome vendors were the *regrattiers*, the fruit and vegetable merchants, who sold also candles and a few household supplies. They came, men and women, accompanied by a boy or two who carried the produce in baskets. There were many other itinerant street merchants who sold everything from needles to soap. Boys struggled along with loads of charcoal in sacks on their backs, and with wood for the fireplaces. The street was too narrow for carts although an occasional one did jog its way through. Most interesting were the wine criers. They had a bowl of fresh wine and a short stick with which to tap it to attract attention. They advertised the latest shipment of wine received at a given tavern. The bleating of sheep and the noises of poultry added to the variety. A hasty bargain could often be made at the door. The coin in daily use was the *denier*, or silver penny, which had in Paris at this date the equivalent of about four cents' worth of our silver in it. Twelve of these *deniers* were a *sou*, roughly equivalent to the amount of silver in our fifty cents. Two thirds of a pound (Troy weight) was a *marc*, about seven dollars in our modern money. This means that a *livre* (Troy weight) was the equivalent of ten dollars in silver value. But the only coins in actual circulation at the time were the *denier*, and sometimes the half *lenier* or *maille*. About 120 *deniers* could be carried in a purse at the belt.

It was customary when a young man enrolled with a teacher for him to permit that master to take charge of his accounts. Mestre Guillaume had a special chest in his *salle* on the *premier*

étage in which he kept small leather bags, each containing the
money of an individual student. The only way accounts could
be kept straight was with the aid of a counting board. This
was a small thin board marked with a "tree," that is, a long
painted line crossed at intervals by long and short bars or lines
which indicated the units, fives, tens, fifties, hundreds, five
hundreds, and so on. When any counting had to be done Guillaume would lay his board on a stool and use the small metal
counters which could be shifted around from one value to another as he added the figures. The totals were noted in Roman
numerals on a vellum sheet which served as a ledger. Perhaps
the master should have been nervous with this small "banking"
business going on in his house, but the stairway tower made his
home into a stronghold. In case of burglary or attack, one
could lock himself in and yell for help. Aid would not be slow
in coming in that sector of the town. The Bishop of Paris had
a long arm, and a sufficient number of serjanz under his *avoué*
or lay administrator who could keep the watch. These men
could be found near the Petit Chastelet, the fortified gate at the
end of Petit Pont, so they were only a few yards from the house
of Guillaume. Nonetheless the rigid separation of justice between civil and ecclesiastical was a pain to the average citizen.
The young prince Phillip had been advised to make an effort to
get the consent of the Bishop for intervention by the king's
serjanz when both laity and clergy (students) were involved
within the gates of Paris proper.

It is now our plan to follow Mestre Guillaume through a
day's routine. There was, of course, no clock in the household.
Time was kept in one of the principal religious communities
with a water clock. The church bells were rung at Sainte Op-
portune, striking the canonical hours: Prime, Terce, Sexte,
None, Vespers, Compline, Matins or Vigils, and Lauds. Sup-
posedly these were three hours apart but, as was the case since
Roman times, the daylight hours were lengthened in the warmer
months, and were shortened in darker seasons. This was a sort
of daylight-saving time. In addition, everyone was made aware
of daybreak when the watchman on the Grant Chastelet gate
blew his horn, and of mid-day, which could be seen by looking
up overhead. Perhaps a curfew bell was rung between Vespers
and Compline (modern seven thirty or eight o'clock). With
this inaccuracy of time no one bothered to live from minute to

minute. Life was more leisurely. You lived from bell to bell, with plenty of time in between.

Mestre Guillaume was accustomed to rising in the morning when the watchman blew the dawn—*corna l'aube*. After putting on his clothes, which had been flung the night before on the foot bar of the bed, he usually made a hasty trip to Saint Julien down the street where he and the family heard Mass. This was not obligatory and was omitted on week days if occasion demanded. On his return the master drank a cup of clabber, or sometimes wine, and then took his place in the only armchair in the class room on the street floor of his house. The students were already there, before it was fully light. This morning session lasted for approximately two hours and was devoted largely to reading and the correcting of student exercises. Latin verse had to be turned into Latin prose, and vice versa, with much paraphrasing. Explanations were interspersed. When all this was over, the students usually remained for private discussions, and there was often business with a father or a patron.

Not long before Sexte (we will say eleven o'clock) the serving boy placed himself in the doorway of the stair tower and announced that the tables were laid above. Mestre Guillaume, maybe accompanied by a guest or two, climbed the stair and took his place in the armchair, back to chimney. The meal was simple. Two people ate from one bowl or *escuelle*, using their fingers, and a knife if required. Guillaume sometimes shared his bowl with a guest, but more often with his wife. Wine was passed around in a large common cup, a *henap*, and this was filled repeatedly from a wine-skin which lay on the end of the table. Where a dish was particularly soft, like a *morterel* or hot bread pudding, spoons were passed around and later carefully counted. A small buffet stood against the wall in which the *henaps* were kept and on which bread or fruit could stand. On a cold day there was very little light in the room, except from the flickering fire, for the twin windows were covered by the green vellum screen, which gave a soft but unearthly tinge to items on the table.

The meal was consumed rather slowly, for about an hour, and then the members of the family took their rest—their Sexte. We have mentioned the bed which remained against the wall. Some preferred to lay a *coute* or padded mattress with bright cover on the brick floor. Often Mestre Guillaume just sat in his chair and read. When using the chair for study he set a reading stand before him which had also a foot rest. There was an ink horn in the stand. At this time the knack of finishing and polishing wood surfaces was not well advanced. A wood surface was more often than not covered with leather or with a cloth. The leather was fastened down firmly with a kind of casein glue. Guillaume's reading stand was covered on the upper surface with a green *burel* of coarse linen weave. The color green was a favorite one about the house. It was recognized that this was easy on the eyes, and eyes were too frequently strained by poor light and the weakness of old age.

When the family rose up again for the second part of the day, it was *relevee* (about one o'clock in our time). They adjusted their dress and the teacher descended for another bout with his students. These young men had bought their food at a cook shop near the Petit Pont and had eaten, and rested afterwards, at the front of the classroom. This second two-hour period was a more exacting one. Sometimes the master would dictate selections from an author who was being studied; at other times there would be a discussion according to the rules of Dialectic. When the students left at None, the immediate business was over for the day. Often master and students repaired to a tavern for a noisy drinking period; or they might go to the quarters of some other master. Students could make their way to the *pré aus clers*, down the Rue de la Huchette, toward the Abbey of Saint-Germain des Prés, for a game of ball or a walk. Supper came at Vespers (six o'clock) and it was a repetition of the dinner. At the end of it the family liked to loll before the fire, if there were one (and there usually was, even in spring and fall). They told stories and sometimes they were lucky enough to have an entertainer in their midst who chanted a Latin *conte* or amusing and sentimental verses. The weaker members of the family retired at a respectable hour but Mestre Guillaume and his student lodgers in the *soler* above often sat up by candle light into the early morning. They were careful to lock with double turn the exit door from the tower into the classroom and Guillaume was not too disturbed when he knew from noises below that some vagrants were lying there out of the wind and weather for the night.

The holidays came with some frequency. On those days

Mestre Guillaume could join his family and friends in being just a plain mediaeval citizen. There were tourneys after Easter, and many clercs did not scorn to be present at some of these, just as modern professors are known to go to football games. When two or three days' rest came together, Guillaume could take advantage of them and pay a visit to Mucegros, his native heath. Travelling on horseback one could make about thirty-five miles in a day, which meant that Guillaume was about a day's journey from his rustic beginnings. His people were well-to-do peasants who dwelt in a fortified manor house. Some income still came to him from this manor and its lands. Most of it was food and clothing which he needed in order to keep his house in order. Pope Alexander had recently issued instructions that the teachers in the Paris schools should no longer charge students for instruction. This was an impossible and intolerable order for masters who were not wealthy. Fees continued to be paid but it was done quietly by deducting from funds left in the master's care. An impecunious student spent about six marcs a year for instruction, board, lodging, and some miscellaneous items. This amounts to about forty-two dollars of our time, which is certainly no large sum. Often the parents or friends of students would bring food and other homely gifts to the master when they came to town. Living was fairly easy.

Mestre Guillaume was proud of his books. They were piled in a chest which stood near the fireplace in the second floor front. Those that were being read currently were heaped beside the reading stand before the armchair. Some of the books were covered with bare wooden bindings; a few had skin glued over the wood; some were bound in parchment. A few had been copied by Guillaume himself, very laboriously. Usually, however, they had been purchased from a local book dealer on order. Some of the dealers rented books also. Most of the copying of Mestre Guillaume, done by candlelight, consisted of excerpts, *florilegia*. Sayings of the rhetoricians and of the grammarians were favorites of his and he frequently used them. It was best to have them bound together. In the fairs at Saint Lazare and of the Lendit, north of the right-bank stockade, Guillaume bought his stock of vellum in May and June. This had to be scraped and pummiced, but this was a task that he knew well how to do. Later he had to cut the sheets into shape and rule them with a lead point.

For news of the day one had to go to the streets and the markets. Emmeline and her upstairs maid were most adept at gathering this, and they regaled the family with it at table. There was much talk at this time about what the English and old King Henry would do, but there was no cause for alarm. Paris was filled with English students, who were rather a decent lot. They were a little noisy, and a little drunken perhaps with their "Drink-hail and Wass-hail," but they were good friends. As a matter of fact, two of the sons of the English king were in Paris much of the time. These were the Young King Henry and Prince Geoffrey. Richard also was occasionally there. It was a shame that Eleanor, the mother, who had once been the Queen of Paris, was now confined at Salisbury and could no longer hold her court at Poitiers. She was a sprightly lady still, despite her years, and she was always the subject of many stories. There was talk of a Crusade, but Henry of England was disposed to do very little about it, although he had taken the Cross in 1177. Feeling against the Jews was beginning to run very high. Phillip, when he became king in fact, would be needing money, and it was thought that exile of the Paris Jews was a good way to get it. There were about two dozen Jewish families who lived in the Rue des Juis on the other end of Petit Pont. Many of them were bakers. Emmeline often passed by there and bought pasties, which were turn-overs of cheese, egg, and peppered eel. Christian bakers made them also from ham. Wafers and waffles were favorites. The pasties were sold in small baskets covered with a white cloth, and Paris was famed for these. Life was pleasant in Paris. Old King Louis, the father of Phillip, used to say: "We do not have much wealth in France; but we have plenty of food—and *joie*."

Sometimes the Guillaume family fell sick, and it is interesting to observe what they did then. All clerics were liable to know something of the rudiments of medicine. They had an *Antidotarium*, or manual of prescriptions, somewhere at hand. For a nervous stomach, which troubled Guillaume, as it does many moderns, he was accustomed to nibbling a handful of spices in the course of the day. If the stomach persisted to the point of pain he would purchase a little mandrake root at the apothecary shop. (Mandragorine is akin to atropine, which is present in belladonna). When the ailment was more serious, or where actual manual skill was required, the goodman called a *mire*.

This physician was a layman who had learned his trade from another man of medicine by apprenticeship; he was fairly reliable. He could set a bone, drain pus from a wound, and apply a plaster with the best of them. Mestre Guillaume's boy had once been afflicted with a scaly skin ailment. The *mire* had applied a salve made from glasswort, olive oil, and vinegar, and the scabs had dropped away. This man knew herbs that were not familiar to Guillaume. But alas, no one in those times knew why teeth were loose and why there were persistent sores that troubled everyone. These were probably due to the absence of vitamin C in the diet. It was only by chance, and a rare chance, that this vitamin was taken, except by the monks and the very poor, who ate a vegetable diet.

The most unfortunate thing for many was the inability to do anything for astigmatism. This nice word was not known to them, of course, but many clercs knew that their sight was getting dimmer and that their eyes were giving pain. The first remedy was to read manuscripts with large lettering. They tried astringent eye washes, but these did very little good. Finally those who were afflicted had to get some other clerc to read for them. Guillaume was already at the larger lettering stage. Fortunately the last stage was being anticipated, for his son had already learned his letters and ciphering, as had his sister. The son would soon be presented to the Bishop, or his vicar, for the simple tonsure, and then he would go to some school like the one that was taught by his father. The mediaeval man preferred, when it was possible, to have his children educated and reared by someone else. This enlarged their horizon and gave other opportunities. Guillaume had in mind a school for the Trivium maintained by the Augustinian canons at Saint Victor, only a few hundred yards away down the Rue de la Boucherie. If the son took a liking to the Augustinian ways, that was so much the better. He might try at a later date to gain admission to that community. This would place him in a higher professional bracket than that of his father. These canons maintained a celebrated school for Theology and Dialectic, which we would call a graduate school. In the meantime the boy would be a help in reading to his father.

The daughter was twelve years of age and could be apprenticed to some fine needlewoman, or she could even learn such a trade as medicine. The *mire* had female assistants who were destined to be *miresses*. But Emmeline hankered to have her daughter just a simple housewife like herself. Since the relatives of both parents were in the country, they had no city household where they could place their daughter, and had followed the unusual practice of letting her remain at home. The upstairs maid was a relative who had pursued the common custom: she had been sent away from home to better herself. A clerical household was not the best place to meet marriageable young men, but both daughter and maid from the country could expect that Mestre Guillaume would arrange their future before long, although the marriage portions would be small.

We hope that this leisurely voyage to Paris of the late twelfth century has shown, among other things, that life could be pleasant in the time of Eleanor of Aquitaine. Few people born into the twentieth century—or even the nineteenth—would wish to have lived seven hundred and fifty years ago. We would not care for the differences in sanitation and food, the lack of privacy, the fondness for crowds and noise, the indifference to minor physical suffering, and the somewhat isolated mental climate which did not permit a man to wonder very much what was on the next street. But a visit as short as ours—a visit for a round of the water clock—allows us to remain immune to all these nuisances.

The Department of Romance Studies Digital Arts and Collaboration Lab at the University of North Carolina at Chapel Hill is proud to support the digitization of the North Carolina Studies in the Romance Languages and Literatures series.

DEPARTMENT OF
Romance Studies
Digital Arts and Collaboration Lab

www.ingramcontent.com/pod-product-compliance
Lightning Source LLC
Chambersburg PA
CBHW021235020726
47498CB00008B/2849